Published by the World Squash Library

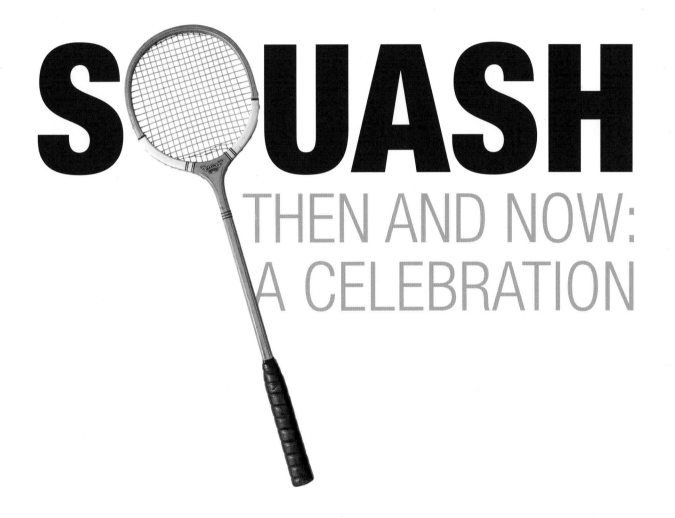

SQUASH
THEN AND NOW:
A CELEBRATION

Andrew Shelley • **Bas van Hoorn**

This first edition published 2024

World Squash Library
ISBN: 978-1-3999-8439-3

The authors have tried to ensure the accuracy of all information, and that the permission of owners of images has been sought as far as possible.

Text: Andrew Shelley and Bas van Hoorn

Design: David O'Connor Designs

Photography: most objects J.P. Krüsemann, most modern by Steve Line

Printed in England: Newman Thomson Printers Ltd.

Order fulfilment: PDH Sports

CONTENTS

FOREWORD: **NICOL DAVID**

In the early stages of my squash journey, the only extent of my knowledge of squash history were some names my dad would talk about, such as Jahangir & Jansher Khan or Michelle Martin and Sarah Fitz-Gerald. As a kid and I didn't really know much about the other players competing on tour.

When time went on and I started to compete for Malaysia, we began to know more former squash champion names like Heather McKay, Susan Devoy, Jonah Barrington and Geoff Hunt as the greats of squash history. It was really difficult to find old videos of squash matches played or articles about these squash greats' journeys as they were not very common in those days.

Of course, luckily for me, when I moved to Amsterdam to work with Liz Irving, I was given plenty of background on the very best squash players through her. So I could learn to emulate them to be the best I can be, and to gain valuable information from her amazing experience of being at the top of the game for so long. She had videos of Susan Devoy, Jahangir Khan and many more for me to watch, analyse and understand what top level squash was all about.

However, I still didn't get to read much about the rich history of squash while I was competing throughout my career. I imagined there would be some books out there giving earlier details but what Andrew and Bas have done is to capture all the details with illustrations and visuals that have been compiled since the very beginning of when squash started.

I have known Andrew since I first started playing junior tournaments in England and also the World Junior tournaments; but as I joined the Women's Tour (WISPA at that time), Andrew was always the person that was our true support system in every way. He cared for us women squash players and did everything in his power to make sure we were looked after on tour. He knew so much about the sport's history since I met him and I loved hearing the stories. I did like asking him to share more whenever we travelled together on our WISPA Promotional and WSF Ambassador tours all around the world. It amazes me how he always remembers everyone, makes an effort to keep the squash community growing and has seen the sport develop with his very own eyes.

That is why it is so fitting to see what Andrew is doing through the World Squash Library to make sure that the history of squash is not forgotten, and this publication brings it to life. I'm truly grateful for his contribution to our sport, and to Bas van Hoorn, a squash history expert and researcher, who has done a great service for the sport by collecting together so many historical rackets, balls and other material that will be brought to life in the book.

This is an incredible initiative by them and they worked really hard to gather important details of our sport through photos and illustrations that we rarely find anywhere in the world, until now.

Now, knowing and understanding more about the generations that came before me in this sport, whatever I have gone through in my squash career is just a small element of the bigger picture that this sport strongly holds onto, and the legacy it will carry on from now.

Thank you Andrew and Bas for putting your heart into this beautiful World Squash Library piece of squash history that will remain with us in our lifetimes.

Nicol David
8 times World champion

FOREWORD: **JONAH BARRINGTON**

I must begin by thanking the inestimable Andrew Shelley and his collaborator Bas van Hoorn for inviting me to write the foreword to this most fascinating publication.

I was recently watching an interview with the amazing Billie Jean King. She was saying that as a youngster she was consumed with the history of her sport. I too, from a very young age, have been drawn to the background (informative) narrative of many different pursuits and squash has obviously had a leading place. I am now at an advanced point in my existence, and while I don't dwell on and draw much from my dwindling memory bank, I still find, through media outlets in the main, the pictures of the past setting thoughts in motion again. I am not presently privy to whether many of the younger squash aficionados wonder too much where their game actually started. How perhaps, as I did, scarcely believe the basic specifications of the court are very much the same as those that were first constructed and laid down in tablets of stone seemingly in 1923.

I am sure, however, that this World Squash Library book will intrigue those who love to delve into this fine pictorial compendium of our so special game. It really is remarkable, quite unlike any other (though I must mention fives of course), steeped in gladiatorial moments and treading a treacherous passage full of impediments to the 2028 Olympics in Los Angeles. Ours has essentially been a hidden, almost secretive activity, but bearing an inner core, never to falter nor disappear off the sporting map.

Andrew Shelley has always loved playing squash despite having a technique that would not have passed muster in the 19th century, let alone since! But his unrivalled knowledge and administrative skills are actually legendary as his adult working pathway has taken him for more than four decades; from the then SRA (now England Squash) to the women's professional organisation (WISPA) and then masterminding the considerable affairs of the world federation (WSF). This prodigious experience is now happily available to ensure that our past is never forgotten.

And with him has been, most interestingly, a Dutchman, Bas van Hoorn, a coach I recall fondly from my time working with the Dutch players, and the most avid of memorabilia collectors. Together they have pieced together this quite remarkable pictorial montage of where it all began and evolved down the ages.

I do feel blessed to have played a part in that long chronicle, and am keeping everything crossed that at least at a distance I can welcome our sport into the Games in 2028. It remains rather a disturbing obsession; I have never lost faith that despite so much trial and tribulation our game would never drift into obscurity despite the perpetual lack of interest from the media. It just has ways of sustaining itself, and at the core have been those like Andrew who have never accepted anything other than the best for squash.

I say once more that we all need to remember from whence we have come and use that knowledge to forge the future. We should all salute Andrew and Bas for this marvellous memorial – and now onwards to the next century of fun!

Jonah Barrington
6 times British Open champion

INTRODUCTION

This book is not intended as an all-encompassing history of squash. It does not attempt to cover every great player of every country, or every major tournament in all eras. Formal histories have already been written, and written very well, by authors such as John Horry, Rex Bellamy and James Zug.

By contrast this book contains hundreds of small historical fragments, scattered visual pieces of a much larger jigsaw, some already well known, others new bits of information. By presenting these pieces in this visual way, we hope it will encourage understanding of, and interest in, the long and rich squash history. Flicking through the pages will offer a glimpse into the development of squash from bygone eras until now. As the title says, it is a celebration of the wonderful history of our sport.

The authors would like to thank everybody who has been involved in the production of this book – which would have been a shadow of itself without them.

David O'Connor instantly committed to using his design expertise to bring the text and images to life superbly. For photographing objects from Bas's collection, and for general photo-editing, we were very lucky to have found Hans Krüsemann, who spared no effort and did such a wonderful job. The unparalleled collection of photos taken by Steve Line in the course of his work covering events for the last four decades has made a huge difference in enlivening later chapters, and is greatly appreciated. www.squashinfo.com proved invaluable for checking player data. Valued help was received from Sarah Wilkinson who proof-read the text; and the partnership with PDH Sports has ensured that the books can reach the hands of readers.

Nicol David and Jonah Barrington, two of the all-time greats of the sport, were so kind to agree to write the forewords; a huge honour, for which we are truly grateful.

Finally, to our financial and family supporters: Barbara Scott and Tom Tarantino from Philadelphia, PA., USA, who underwrote the project. Thank you to all who have contributed to the production of the book; including the family and friends of the authors who gave them support and the space to create it!

Notes:

If, despite the efforts of the authors, any errors have slipped through, please inform them so that corrections can be made in future editions.

Over time both racquets and rackets have been used as part of the name of the sport, but here rackets has been used to standardise it.

THE AUTHORS

Andrew Shelley has been involved in squash administration and management since 1976. For 18 years he managed events and operations, including the British Open, for the English SRA. From 1994 until 2010 he was CEO of WISPA (the women's pro tour). Following that he became CEO of the World Squash Federation until 2019, at which point he retired and founded the World Squash Library to 'give back' to the sport. He also acted as Championship and Technical Director for many world championships; and was awarded an MBE for services to squash in 2021.

He is immensely grateful to his wife and family who have allowed him a lifetime selfishly dedicated to squash!

Bas van Hoorn (born 1971) is a former squash coach from the Netherlands. He has coached professional players on the world tour; notably his sister, Hugoline van Hoorn, and Annelize Naude (during the later stage of her career). For nearly thirty years he has been researching the history of squash (especially pre-1960s) and its forerunners. During this time he has built a world-renowned collection of squash and rackets memorabilia. Many of these items are presented in this book for the first time.

Bas would like to dedicate this book: *To my mother who taught me the love for history, to my father who taught me the love for sports, to my aunts Emmy & Cookje who were my extra mums, to my sister Hugoline who has been there for me from the day I was born (and vice versa ;-), to Annelize who I've had the honour to also coach, to Ellen who is my favourite sister-in-law, and to Koen who is the very best best friend one can have.*

Bas coaching his sister Hugoline at the 1995 British Open.

CHAPTER 1

BEFORE SQUASH

Squash comes from a long lineage of sports played with a racket. Before squash, there was the game of rackets. Before rackets there was real tennis. Real tennis was already played in the 13th century, and rackets can also be traced back several hundred years. Squash would, after its birth in the 19th century, continue to be modelled on its parent game rackets until the early 1900s, by which time squash had outgrown its forerunners.

BEFORE SQUASH

Real tennis

Real tennis is the father of all western racket sports. It can be traced back to at least the 13th century. Real tennis is believed to originate in France, where it is called 'jeu de paume' (the palm game) because at first it was played with the hand. In the late 15th century players started using tennis rackets instead, and soon after that the net was also introduced. By then this very popular sport had already spread throughout western Europe. It was usually played on a four-walled court. The opponents face each other on either side of a net. All walls are in play, as is the sloping roof of the spectators gallery, onto which the ball is served. After the 18th century its popularity waned, and today the game is played on about 50 real tennis courts worldwide. In the US it is known as court tennis, and in Australia as royal tennis.

▲ The first printed real tennis image (1497). Note the absence of a net and the lack of rackets as players struck the ball with their gloved hand. Betting on sports was already popular, so the spectator on the left is holding a large purse.

◄ Real tennis scene from France (1552). This shows players using rackets and a net, in the primitive form of a cord.

◄ The first book on the game of real tennis (1555) written by the Italian Antonio Scaino, a theologian and priest, and titled (translated in English) 'Treatise on the game of the ball'.

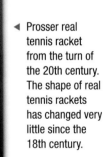

▲ University students playing real tennis in Leiden, Netherlands (1612).

◄ Prosser real tennis racket from the turn of the 20th century. The shape of real tennis rackets has changed very little since the 18th century.

◄ View of an 18th century French real tennis court, of the jeu quarré type. It's not difficult to imagine how some form of front wall game (like the game of rackets) could also be played on tennis courts shaped like this.

Rackets origins

The game of rackets, unlike real tennis, is played against a high front wall instead of over a net. It is a very fast game, played with a small hard leather ball on a court the size of three squash courts but much higher. Most historians agree that rackets originates from the real tennis court. There all requisites for the game would have been readily available. John Davies, the first known indoor rackets champion (c1780-1800) worked as marker at the real tennis court in St.James Street in London, a later example of the ties between the two games.

Another early game closely related to rackets is fives. Also a front wall game, but fives is not played with a strung racket but by hand (it was likely named after the five fingers). Large fives/handball courts, whether open or covered, would have been equally suited for the game of rackets. Rackets in more primitive forms was probably played in England even before the 18th century. In these early stages it usually still went by the name of the other related games, and so it was played on tennis, fives, handball or ball courts. It was not until the late 18th century that it would clearly establish its own name and identity.

▲ Rackets was first played at real tennis courts, like this court in London located at Leicester Fields (1788).

▲ A 17th century token issued by a merchant *'at the Racket'* '*in Fleet Street*' in London. For many centuries an alleyway was located there called 'Racquet Court', which can be traced back to at least 1622, when the area was known for its taverns with manly sports.

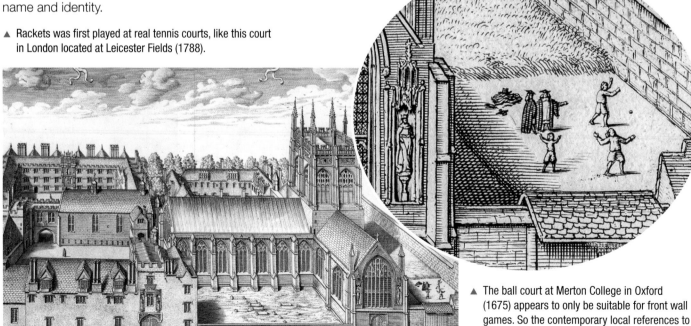

▲ The ball court at Merton College in Oxford (1675) appears to only be suitable for front wall games. So the contemporary local references to *'tennis'* seem to indicate instead that the game of rackets in some early form was played there, besides the depicted handball/fives.

► Rackets was also played on fives courts, like this large covered court (1821), probably in Little St. Martin's Street, London, a court which existed from the early 1700s and was known not only for rackets but also for boxing matches.

▲ A game of rackets in the courtyard of the Fleet Prison in London, from 'the Humours of the Fleet' (1749), a pamphlet about life in the debtors' prison.

Prison rackets

In the London debtors' prisons rackets became recognised for the first time as an independent sport. First mentioned in the 1740s in the Fleet Prison, from then on we begin to find occasional references to the prison game. Like in 1767 when in the King's Bench a match at rackets (at that time often still called fives) was played, a handicap contest with one player wearing on his legs a pair of iron shackles. Or in 1793 when three prisoners tried to escape from the Bench while most of the guards were busy playing rackets.

▲ A thirsty rackets player entering a 'whistling shop', a room in the Fleet Prison where spirits were privately sold. Original sketchbook drawing (detail) by the caricaturist George Cruikshank (1820).

Popular London sites

By 1800 the game was firmly established. At that time these prisons were peculiar, lively places. Most prisoners were not locked up in their rooms and many had their families living with them. Outsiders could walk in and out, and the prisons became popular London sites. There was a coffee house, some rooms had shops, spirits were sold, and the Fleet was even called the largest brothel in London.

There were four open rackets courts in the King's Bench, and in the Fleet at least two. The racket masters were prisoners, who received fees for hiring out the court and equipment. Some earned enough to pay off all their debts. Players were outsiders as well as prisoners. The early champions of the open court had apparently all learned the game while living there. Matches for high stakes were regularly held between the top players, often in front of a large crowd. And so rackets thrived there until the 1840s. Then, due to prison reforms, the Fleet was demolished, and in the, by then, Queen's Bench from 1850 outsiders were no longer allowed to play.

▲ John Mitchell, who as a child had learned to play rackets in the King's Bench Prison. During the 1840s and 1850s he reigned as British (de facto world) rackets champion, in both the open court and the indoor variant.

▶ Rackets played on two of the open courts in the King's Bench Prison (c1820).

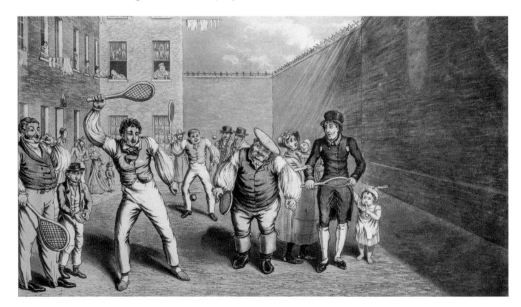

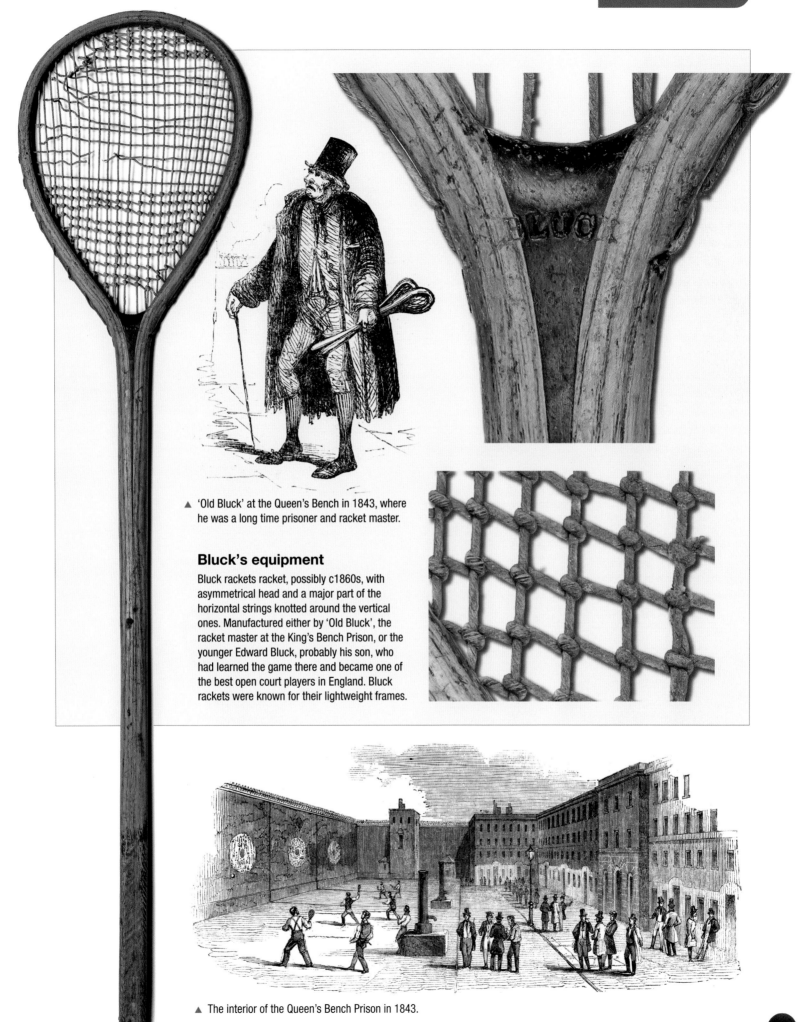

▲ 'Old Bluck' at the Queen's Bench in 1843, where he was a long time prisoner and racket master.

Bluck's equipment

Bluck rackets racket, possibly c1860s, with asymmetrical head and a major part of the horizontal strings knotted around the vertical ones. Manufactured either by 'Old Bluck', the racket master at the King's Bench Prison, or the younger Edward Bluck, probably his son, who had learned the game there and became one of the best open court players in England. Bluck rackets were known for their lightweight frames.

▲ The interior of the Queen's Bench Prison in 1843.

Pub games

The taverns, together with the debtors' prisons, were the strongholds of rackets during the first half of the 19th century. In London there were a number of public houses with open rackets courts. Working class Londoners would walk there in the evening or on Sundays for a pint and a game. The most famous was the Belvidere Tavern, built around 1780, with its pleasure gardens. Its rackets court at first consisted of *'a simple boarded hoarding'* but in 1820 this was replaced by a more elaborate court. In 1838 John Lamb beat John Pittman there for the championship. In the decades that followed all matches for the Open court championship of Britain would be held at the Belvidere.

▲ Rackets at the Belvidere Tavern in London (1858).

Not only in London but throughout the country rackets was played at taverns. Usually outdoors but sometimes also on covered courts like in Birmingham and Bristol. It was not until the 1860s that the popularity of the tavern game began to wane. In London and other major cities more and more open courts were demolished, also due to the ever expanding urban redevelopments, and within a few decades the tavern game would die out all together.

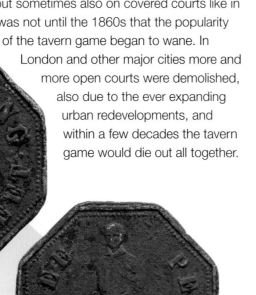

▲ Three pence token of Samuel Young (depicted) the champion player at the covered Racket Court at the Bath Street Inn, Birmingham (c1860).

▲ Frank Erwood, British indoor rackets champion from 1860-1862. Also an excellent open court player, he is apparently the last champion who had learned the game in a debtors' prison.

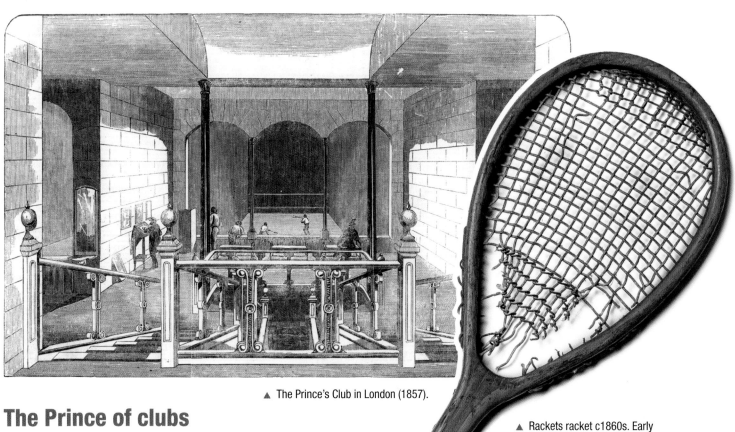

▲ The Prince's Club in London (1857).

The Prince of clubs

By 1850 rackets in England had already been played indoors in some form for a long time. Not just on covered real tennis and fives courts, but also on indoor courts built specifically for rackets: like at some Birmingham taverns, or at Woolwich for the Royal Artillery (1830s) or at Lord Eglinton's Castle (c1840). But it really took off as indoor sport when the exclusive Prince's Club in London opened in 1856. This proved a turning point in rackets history. The club had no less than seven covered courts, and the size of its match court (60x30 feet) is still the standard today. Annual championships were instituted by the club for the universities, the public schools and, later, the military. These groups soon began to build similar (indoor) rackets courts elsewhere. This coincided with the decline of the open courts which had already set in, and from then on rackets would rapidly become an indoor game for the upper classes.

▲ Rackets racket c1860s. Early heavy racket, unmarked, from a time when the game was still often played outdoors.

▲ In 1860 Rugby was (one of) the first school(s) to build a covered rackets court. The attached open fives courts would a few years later serve as the inspiration for the first squash courts built at Harrow.

▶ Gold enameled stick pin in the shape of a rackets racket with a pearl as ball. Produced c1865 by the prestigious British goldsmiths London & Ryder.

▼ The first book on the game of rackets (1872) came in a luxurious binding. It was written by J.R. Atkins, a civil servant and enthusiastic amateur player.

▲ A game of rackets at Oxford University (c1860).

▶ The final of the Public Schools rackets championship at Prince's Club in 1875.

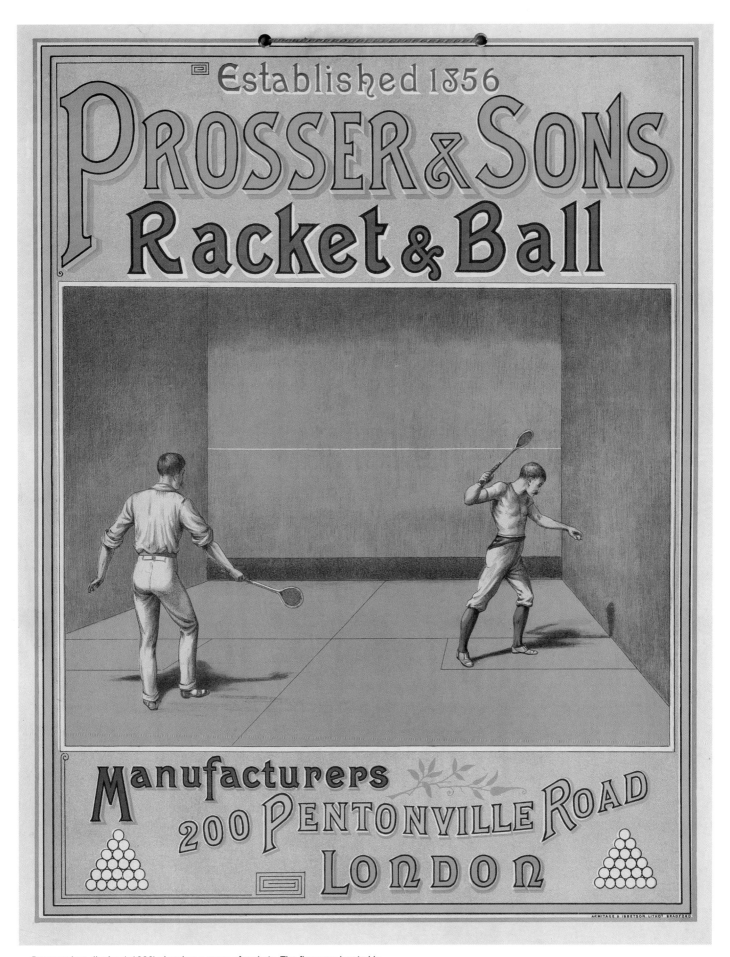

▲ Prosser shop display (c1880) showing a game of rackets. The firm was located in the same street as the Belvidere Tavern and rackets court.

Rackets at Harrow School

Rackets was played at Harrow by at least the late 18th century. At first against the walls of the school building, and later also against a high wall surrounding the school yard. In 1850 two courts were built specifically for rackets, both still open-air and one lacking a side wall. These soon became old fashioned, especially after the London Prince's Club and also Rugby School started playing rackets on indoor courts.

So Harrow built its own covered rackets court, which was officially opened in January 1865. Three years later the Public Schools rackets championship was first held at Prince's. Representing the school there was held in high regard by the Harrow boys, and rackets continued to be an important and popular school sport. During the 19th century in particular no school was more successful at rackets than Harrow. This was often attributed to the fact that the younger Harrow pupils first played squash. At that time squash was considered merely a pastime, but useful practice for the parent sport rackets. Today at Harrow rackets is still played on two covered courts.

▲ Harrow pupils playing rackets against the wall of the school building (1795).

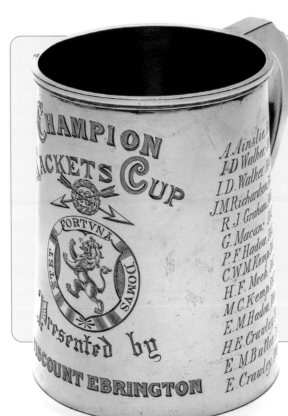

Harrow prizes

Two Harrow rackets trophies: a pewter tankard for the Harrow four wall racquet competition (1859) when the game was still only played outdoors there; and a silver trophy, the Ebrington cup, engraved with the names of the Harrow School champions from 1858 to 1886.

◄ Scenes at the Public Schools rackets championship of 1888, when Harrow played against Eton.

► 'Judy' Stevens (c1880), rackets pro at Harrow School from 1877-1909. He also taught his nephew, Charles Read, the first great squash champion.

◄ Carte de Visite photograph of M.C. Kemp (left) and F. de Moleyns, the Harrow pair that won the Public Schools rackets championship in 1879.

Rackets abroad

Rackets also spread abroad. In India it was played by British officers as early as the 18th century. In the 1780s Colonel John Mordaunt, described as a *'master of his racket'*, played at the large (90x40 feet) fives court in Lucknow. Other early fives/rackets courts were located at Madras, Vellore, and at the Calcutta Racket Club (founded in 1793). Rackets remained popular with the British in India throughout the 19th and early 20th centuries.

Many garrisons were stationed at the northern frontier, in what is now Pakistan, where a number of courts were built for the officers. Local men who were hired there were introduced to the sport this way. In the 20th century some of their descendants would become the great Khan squash champions. During the 19th century rackets was also played in Ireland, where there seems to have existed an older tradition of rackets play in some form, but it's unclear how far back that goes. In other countries, like Scotland, Hong Kong, Australia, the USA and Canada rackets was played too, imported there by the English.

▲ A morning scene in the daily life of the British in India in 1842 - the unequal colonial relations depicted is rightly considered unacceptable today. For one of the British leisure activities a rackets racket is shown front right.

▲ In 1867 William Gray (left) the champion from England played Fred Foulkes (right). Foulkes was American champion and the first challenger from outside the British Isles, but lost this international match for 1,000 GBP. William was one of three brothers Gray who were world rackets champions. His brother Henry held the title before him and founded the Grays racket manufacturing firm in Cambridge, still in existence today.

▲ The Duke of Wellington (future hero of the Waterloo battlefield, but at the time a Colonel) lost this gold mounted walking stick to his fellow officer Lt. Anthony Weldon (4th Bart, 1781-1858) in a rackets match in India in 1801.

◄ Group of British rackets players in Coimbatore together with the Indian marker in traditional dress c1870s.

▲ Rackets courts at Calcutta c1908. Most courts in India were open-air which were better suited for the climate.

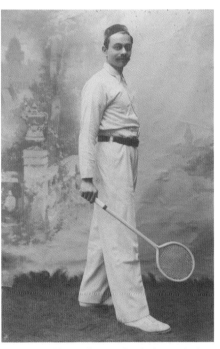

▲ Jamsetji Merwanji was a Parsi who worked as rackets marker at the Bombay Gymkhana. He was world rackets champion from 1903 to 1911.

◄ A different kind of ball in the rackets court at the Toronto Club in 1871. Both in Canada and the US the game can be traced back to at least the late 18th century.

THE RACKETS CHAMPIONSHIP OF THE WORLD, FOR £2,000.

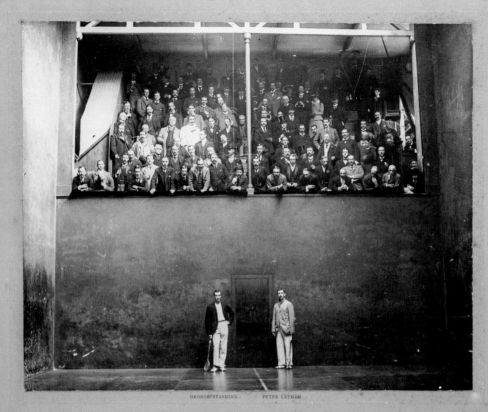

First Match,
OCTOBER 16, 1897.

Played at Queen's Club,
West Kensington.

WON BY
PETER LATHAM.
4 GAMES TO 1.

THE GAMES WERE: 15-11, 15-13, 15-10, 15-18, 15-4, giving Latham an advantage of 19 aces and setting Standing the task, in order to win the Championship, of winning the second match either by 4 games to 0 or 4 games to 1. In the latter case it would be necessary for Standing to gain a majority of more than 19 aces. This, it will be seen, was not accomplished.

Second Match,
NOVEMBER 27, 1897.

Played at New York
Rackets and Tennis Club.

WON BY
PETER LATHAM.
4 GAMES TO 3.

THE GAMES WERE: 15-2, 16-18, 3-15, 16-15, 9-15, 17-16, 15-1. The Championship was actually decided when, in the second match, Latham had secured two games (as Standing could not then win by so much as 4 to 1), which happened at the fourth game, Latham taking 1st and 4th and Standing 2nd and 3rd; but, as each had been backed apart from the Championship to win the match in New York, the games were continued until one had won four.

GEORGE STANDING.   PETER LATHAM.

BETWEEN
PETER LATHAM AND GEORGE STANDING
(ENGLAND)   (NEW YORK).

Latham retained his title of Champion by 6 games to 3 and 125 aces to 106, a difference of 19 aces, all gained in the first match. The first four games played in the second match (which decided the Championship) resulted in the players making exactly 50 aces each. Of the whole number of games played, Latham won 8 to 4 and 166 aces to 138.

▲ Mounted photograph of the World rackets championship in 1897. Peter Latham (pro at the Queen's Club, London) beat his challenger George Standing (pro at the Racquet and Tennis Club, NY) in this home and away match.

◄ Rackets in New York in 1876 at the opening of the new club at 26th Street, the forerunner of the present Racquet and Tennis Club.

► The amateur championship at the Queen's Club (1905).

The exclusive game

During the second half of the 19th century the transition of rackets to an indoor sport for the upper classes continued. It was primarily played at public schools, universities, army courts and private clubs, and for a while rackets flourished there. But by 1900 its decline had already set in. One problem was the high cost of building courts and of equipment (balls and wooden rackets needed constant replacing). But the real blow was the rapid advance of squash. By the turn of the century squash was already surpassing its parent game in terms of popularity and number of courts. And while squash continued to grow, rackets was destined to become a minor sport little known to the general public. Today it is played at about 35 covered courts worldwide: more than 20 courts at British public schools, the others mostly at private clubs in the UK, Canada and the United States.

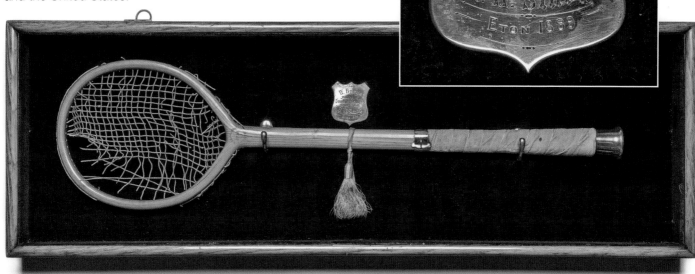

▲ Silver mounted presentation racket in its original case, presented to Walter Burns for winning the Eton doubles rackets championship in 1889.

▲ Eton rackets cap awarded to Hugh S. Gladstone for being one of the 'choices': one of the school's best players that year (1895/96).

▲ Original artwork (1911) of Charles Williams winning the World rackets championship. He would hold the title from 1911-13 and 1929-35.

CHAPTER 2

SQUASH FROM THE BEGINNINGS TO 1920

After its invention by schoolboys at Harrow during the 19th century, squash began to spread. The upper classes started building courts at their homes, at military stations and at clubs, not only in England but all over the world. Still a pastime played under varied conditions, after 1900 the first feeble attempts at standardisation began, inspired by popularisers like Eustace Miles.

SQUASH FROM THE BEGINNINGS TO 1920

Coming out of school

Harrow School, a public school for boys founded in 1572 and located in Harrow, north-west of London, England is where squash originated. In the first half of the 19th century the older sport of rackets was very popular there. Playing time in the rackets courts was in general only available to the oldest boys, who had preferential rights. So the younger pupils invented their own game instead, using a cut-down rackets racket and a 'squashier' ball. They played it in the courtyards of their boarding houses and called it squash.

Each courtyard had its own rules for obstacles as rain pipes, wired windows, doorways (a let) and even recessed foot scrapers (a point). A second side wall was often lacking. The ball was usually made of India rubber, which was facilitated by the invention of rubber-vulcanisation in 1839.

For the first few decades squash remained this primitive Harrow courtyard game under differing conditions. Then Sir William Hart Dyke, a former student, stepped in. He had recently, in 1862, won the world championship at rackets. He was unhappy with the condition of the open rackets courts at his old school.

◄ Sir William Hart Dyke, world rackets champion in 1862.

▲ Boys playing squash at Harrow School in the courtyard of their boarding house, on a contrived court with only one side-wall, and obstacles such as ledges, windows and foot scrapers.

Funds were raised for a better, covered rackets court which was built in 1864, costing £1,600. The donations had exceeded this, and it was decided to spend the extra money on building seven small open-air sports courts: apparently four for the Eton fives (hand ball) game, and three for the recently invented courtyard game of squash. Still open air, but now with the plain walls that we still know today, and to be used with the already familiar cut-down rackets and India rubber balls.

So, Hart Dyke erected the first ever specifically built squash courts at Harrow School. The three courts were opened in January 1865, and so became the milestone of Harrow presiding over the formal birth of the sport.

Harrow pupils already took their racket sports seriously at a young age!

▲ The rackets court at Harrow in 1865 with the new buildings of the open squash courts on the right, the first ever specifically constructed for the game.

▲ A postcard view of Harrow from around 1910 with sports buildings in the middle foreground, including the large indoor rackets court (with turret) and the adjacent uncovered squash courts from 1865.

Other schools

Other schools in the UK started taking up squash after the 'official' birth in 1865 at Harrow. Often on outdoor courts, with no back walls, suitable for both squash and the older (hand ball) game of rugby fives, which required a similarly sized court. Some schools already had such courts in place for fives, which were soon appropriated for squash too. Like at Rugby School, where as early as 1868, a pupil was reported to be worried that the new squash game would replace the older fives.

During the later part of the 19th century many schools started building new courts specifically for squash. The prep school of Elstree, north of London, traditionally had close ties with Harrow as many pupils went there before coming to Harrow. So it's no surprise squash became popular there too (photo). Many other schools followed, like the otherwise little known Hildersham House School in Broadstairs, Kent (postcard). And this very early trophy - the Squash Rackets Challenge Cup - was won by 'Gussy' (Augustus Charles) Oppenheim, aged 12, in December 1895, probably in his last year of preparatory school before he went to Eton.

▲ Elstree School courts.

▲ Hildersham House, Kent.

Home matches

In 1883 Augustus George Vernon Harcourt, a scientist and Old Harrovian, built what is thought to be the first squash court in a home at his Cowley Grange house (present day part of St. Hilda's College) in Oxford. Harcourt raised ten children there, eight girls and two boys, including his son Simon who recounted *'As soon as they could walk … his children were taught the game'.* But not only Harcourt's family members learned squash there. *'Many of his pupils found, to their surprise, that their white-haired tutor could give them lessons in other things besides chemistry'.* And so many Oxford students were first introduced to squash at this home court.

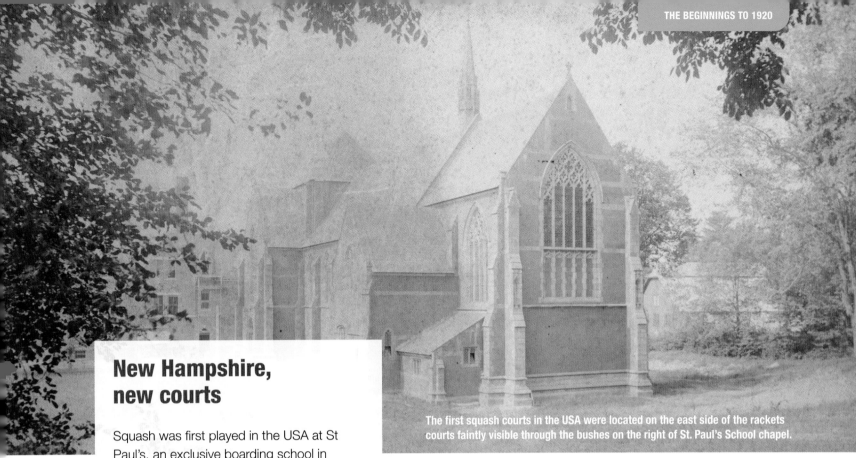

The first squash courts in the USA were located on the east side of the rackets courts faintly visible through the bushes on the right of St. Paul's School chapel.

New Hampshire, new courts

Squash was first played in the USA at St Paul's, an exclusive boarding school in Concord, New Hampshire. It was introduced there by Reverend Jay Conover, a teacher and former student. He was a great sports enthusiast, who was also responsible for first importing ice hockey to the US. In 1884 Conover supervised the building of four squash courts at the school. They were open to air, lacked a back wall, and are said to follow the Harrow dimensions. From rural New Hampshire, boys who had played squash at this elitist school radiated into the cities and soon more courts were being built in North America.

Squash appears in print

June 1894 saw the first magazine article devoted to squash. It appeared in the British Boys Own Paper alongside other stories such as *'a plunge into the Sahara'*, *'how submarine cables are made'*, and *'Indian soldiers at play'*! Written by Somerville Gibney, a former Harrow pupil, it was two pages of closely typed information about squash and how it was played. Unattractively presented in dense wording, but a step forward in raising the profile of the nascent sport.

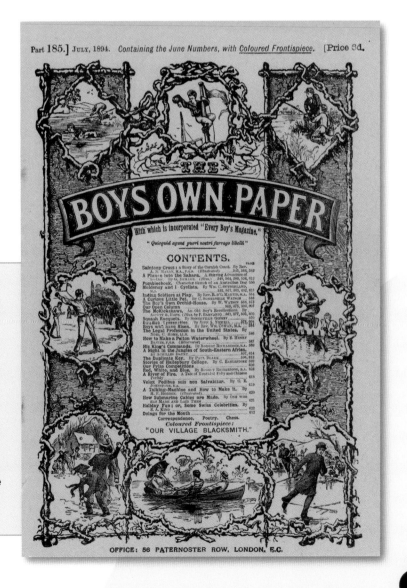

Into the Empire

The former public schoolboys and university students grew up, and became the civil servants and army officers that ruled the British Empire. They spread all over the globe, and by the end of the 19th and the early 20th centuries they started building squash courts wherever they went. Sizes varied, open or enclosed courts, cement or wooden floors, brickwork, wooden or plaster walls, just about everything went, as long as they could continue to play their favorite game while away from home.

Canada

In Canada the first courts appear to have been built at private homes in the late 1800s, as in Vancouver in 1892. Club courts soon followed, like at St John's, Newfoundland (1904) or at the Toronto Racquet Club (1905), with this wooden court.

Switzerland

Even outside the Empire, the British took their squash with them. In 1894 in St. Moritz, Switzerland, a squash court was built at the local skiing resort for the use of the English hotel guests.

South Africa

In South Africa what is assumed to be the first squash court was built at the Johannesburg Country Club in 1906. The court was open to the skies and had a concrete floor. As for size, it was wider than what later became the standard, until in 1930 it was resized and a roof and wooden floor were added. Could the person in front with a wooden leg be the squash court attendant?

India and Pakistan

In India (including present Pakistan), the 'Jewel in the Crown' of the Empire, British clubs sprouted across the country, many including squash courts. For instance in Ootacamund, a hill station in Tamil Nadu, there were two squash courts in play by 1891, at the local club and at the government house. Another early court was at the Adyar Club near Madras (now Chennai). The club was founded in 1890 and was already holding a squash tournament in 1900 featuring this silver miniature jug.

Sudan and Egypt

In Sudan, in Wadi Halfa, squash courts were reported to be in play by the late 1890s.

Similarly in Egypt, squash was introduced for British Empire visitors such as the army. In Cairo in 1882 the Gezira Sporting Club opened (initially called Khedivial), and open-air squash courts were in play there - certainly by 1897. At first used by British members and their guests, but later local Egyptians started trying the sport too, and the rest is history, literally!

New Zealand

Squash first came ashore in New Zealand in the city of Christchurch, on the South Island. It was played on a wooden court built around 1907. The Christchurch Club replaced it with a standard one in 1928. Meanwhile, North Island saw its first court in 1913, when the national capital had one built in Government House. It is still there (pictured) but used for storage and basketball now.

Thailand

Thailand's first squash court was built in 1898 at the Chiang Mai Gymkhana Club, made entirely from teak! The court was demolished in the 1980s after almost 90 years of use. The Royal Bangkok Sports Club (pic) opened in 1901 and also included squash.

These are just a few random examples of how by the late 19th century the English started to spread the game around the globe.

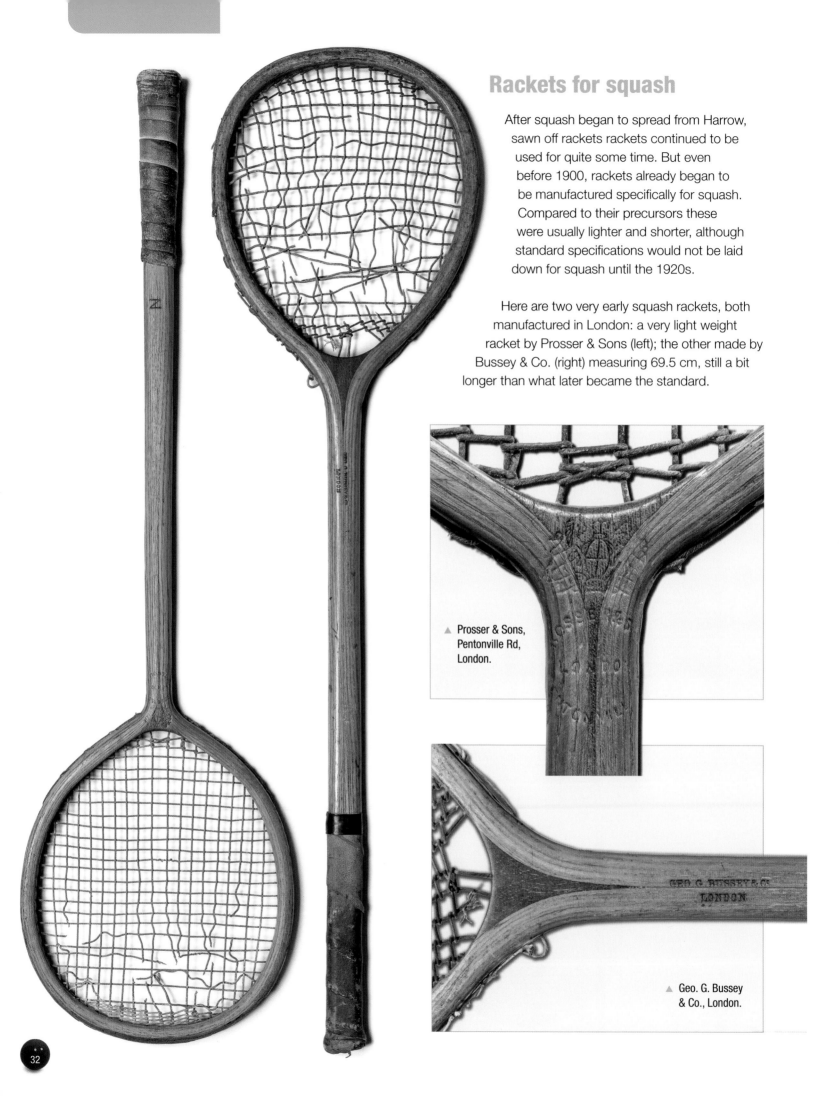

Rackets for squash

After squash began to spread from Harrow, sawn off rackets rackets continued to be used for quite some time. But even before 1900, rackets already began to be manufactured specifically for squash. Compared to their precursors these were usually lighter and shorter, although standard specifications would not be laid down for squash until the 1920s.

Here are two very early squash rackets, both manufactured in London: a very light weight racket by Prosser & Sons (left); the other made by Bussey & Co. (right) measuring 69.5 cm, still a bit longer than what later became the standard.

▲ Prosser & Sons, Pentonville Rd, London.

▲ Geo. G. Bussey & Co., London.

Miles ahead of the rest

Eustace Miles may not be well known today but he was a visionary squash pioneer. In 1901 he published the first ever book about the game. At the time squash was often still regarded as a mere pastime for boys, but Miles began promoting it as a serious sport. An imaginative author, he even included a chapter on *'handicaps'*, suggesting various possible restrictions for the stronger player. It makes Miles the first squash coach to use conditioned games!

A real champion

Miles (1868-1948) was educated at Marlborough College, where he already played squash, before going to Cambridge. An intellectual, he would write over 70 books on subjects as varied as philology, lawn tennis, the history of Rome, food etc. At sports he became hugely successful too, not just squash: he won many major championships at rackets and at real tennis. A bit of an all-rounder! Miles was far ahead of his time: very unusual in this amateur era, he planned his training methodologically, using off court exercises, *'a balanced meatless diet'* (he hated the term vegetarianism), even mind training. His playing style was well thought out too. Although at the start of the century there was no official championship yet, at squash Miles was described as: *'a player without notable natural aptitude who eventually became a real champion'*.

▲ Miles (seen on the back) was the best amateur real tennis player in the world; British & American champion, and winner of the 1908 Olympic silver medal (losing the final to a man that Miles had taught to play).

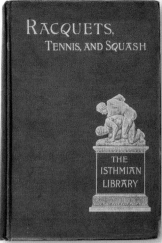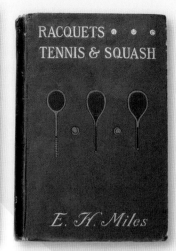

▲ Miles published the first ever book on squash in 1901 (bottom row: US edition left, UK right). He also included squash in a large volume on rackets and real tennis in 1902/3 (top row).

▲ Self-protection!

Miles demonstrating his self-designed ball game apparatus, for training at home.

▲ Pewter squash trophy won by Eustace Miles while studying at King's College, Cambridge in 1892.

Squash goes clubbing

An important step in the development of squash was when the London clubs started adding squash courts to their facilities. By the turn of the century, the former squash playing pupils from the public schools and universities were old enough to have become men of influence. At their London clubs, as elsewhere, they began to build squash courts. Among the first clubs were Lord's (building the court started in 1898), the Bath Club (1904), Queen's (1905), Prince's (in play by 1907) and the Royal Automobile Club (1911). Some of these were sports clubs, but many were West End social clubs. One thing all these luxurious London clubs had in common was that their members were all from the upper classes. When the Bath Club was founded, its aim had been to become *'exclusive, fashionable and aristocratic'*. Those characteristics describe all these London clubs, and indeed the amateur squash players of this era.

The Bath Club at Dover Street was one of the exclusive London clubs which built squash courts at the start of the 20th century. In 1905 the renowned Bath Club handicap tournament was instituted. The club soon became the strongest and most influential squash club in the UK.

▲ Squash was a core activity at the RAC in London from the opening in 1911. There were three courts in the basement of their Pall Mall clubhouse, all narrower in size than what would later become the standard.

Varied conditions

Their courts were all enclosed, but otherwise conditions between these London clubs varied enormously: each club had its own court size, and its own type of ball, the squash rules not having been standardised yet. Club tournaments were held for their own members, like the Bath Club handicap tournament. Playing on another club's court would have felt like playing a different sport altogether, which hampered attempts to organise matches between clubs. As early as 1909 the Bath Club offered a cup for a London inter-club competition, but nothing came of it at the time. There were some exchanges, but only very occasionally, for example in 1908 when a team from Queen's were badly beaten by the Bath Club, the strongest club in the UK. Or when the occasional match for a purse was arranged between two professional coaches from different clubs, the money having been subscribed by their respective members. Like in 1913, when Oak Johnson (the RAC coach) played and lost the match against Charles Read, pro at Queen's and already the best player in England. But these sporadic initiatives would not develop into official competitions until the 1920s, also due to the first World War (1914-1918) when everything came to a standstill.

▲ The squash players of the elitist London clubs knew how to enjoy luxury, like at the RAC where the members naturally had to have a smoking room and even their own cigar stall!

Best foot forward

Even though almost none of the London clubs accepted women as members in the first decade of the 1900's, the Bath Club did. That said, they were not permitted to use the main entrance! Once on court, as these photos (1905) of Miss Ponsonby (left) and Miss Muir-Mackenzie show, footwear was clearly not sporty!

An early 20th century Prosser & Sons squash racket from the prestigious Prince's Club in Knightsbridge, London.

The best players in England during the 1910s were pro* at the London clubs:		
Charles Arnold	Bath Club	From c1911
G. Bannister	Bath Club	Left in 1913 to Hamilton, Canada
Charles Hull	Prince's Club	Lost his leg in WW1
Oak Johnson	RAC	From 1911
Charles Read	Queen's Club	From 1906

*The leading amateur player of this era was Jimmy Palmer-Tomkinson, a member of the Bath Club.

Silver luxury

Silver trophy from 1908 made by Mappin & Webb, the famous UK silversmiths. Trophies with a base of three crossed stems formed as miniature sports equipment like rowing oars, golf clubs or tennis rackets, were regularly produced in the 19th and 20th century, but this is a rare example for squash.

Wooden rackets could warp so presses were introduced to store them between use. Not just single ones, but heavy-duty maximum six racket ones too!

▶ Three very early squash balls (left to right): a Prosser & Sons, best quality no.2B ball (3.8 cm); an unnamed very small (3.4 cm) ball, orange/red with matt finish, solid with an ear in it; and another unnamed ball (3.6 cm), solid with ear and black. All dating from around 1900-1920.

Squash balls

The squash balls that the boys at Harrow used were made of India rubber. Other than that, there are many diverging reports about their further specifications: hollow or hard and solid, punctured or even-surfaced, from *'rather smaller than a fives ball'* to *'about 2 1/4 in. in diameter'*, and from *'fast and yet did not bounce too high'* to *'a very slow affair'*. Even the colours varied; and so during those early years many different types of ball seem to have been used at Harrow.

Once other schools, universities and clubs started taking up squash in the later 19th century, even until the 1920s there were still no specifications for a standard ball laid down. The different rubber balls tended to be chosen by players depending upon the varying conditions of their court. For example at the London Bath Club with its regular sized courts a large ball of c1 11/16 inch (c4.3 cm) was used, the 'holer', so called because it had a small hole in it which made it less bouncy and easier to kill; its colour was usually black, but it was also available in grey and red. By contrast the players at the large squash court at Lord's used a very small, fast ball, which was (nearly) solid. The solid balls had a rubber ear in them, which tended to become loose and rattle inside the ball after a short time in play. All these differences in balls and courts made for a huge variety of squash play.

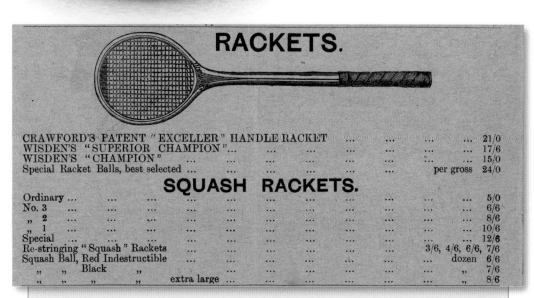

Advertisement from the trade catalogue for 1900 of John Wisden & Co, cricketing, football & lawn tennis manufacturers. At the time Wisden were producing five types of squash racket, and three different squash balls.

America

America's first champions

The USA was the first country in the world to hold a national championship for squash. It started in 1907, and was organised by the United States Squash Racquets Association, which had been founded only three years before. National in name, but at first mostly Philadelphians only, as many of the early winners came from that city. These included William Freeland, who was awarded this runner-up trophy in 1910, having won the championship the previous year. He lost to his great rival, John Miskey, from the Overbrook Golf Club in Greater Philadelphia who would win three of the first four titles.

Another Philadelphian winner was Morton 'Mort' Lewis Newhall (pictured) US National champion in 1913. It was not until 1928 that the women's title was also contested. Both events were played with the hardball until 1990 when the US was switching to the international softball squash game.

An American perspective

Frederick Tompkins, instructor at the Racquet Club of Philadelphia wrote this in 1909: *'The reason that squash in America is so far in advance of England regarding the game is that the courts have been built later and are of a more regulation size, and again America has a more regular set of rules; whereas in England the courts are very different in size and the rules differ very much'*.

From the 1920s onwards, this actually became a disadvantage for the American game, when the UK finally agreed on (different) standard rules for court size/ball type etc, which were followed throughout the rest of the world, and so the North American game became an isolated, different type of squash, called hardball.

▶ US Nationals runner-up trophy 1910.

Locals go national

The Philadelphia Inter-Club Competition was initiated in 1903 between seven clubs from the area. The next year the same seven local clubs formed the United States Squash Racquets Association, the first national federation in the world. Their first logo is shown here as plaque on a trophy awarded by the newly founded USSRA to the winners of the Philadelphian Inter-Club competition in 1907.

Scot conquers America

The best of the early squash players in America was in fact Scottish born. Jock Soutar had been rackets pro at the Prince's Club in London, before crossing the Atlantic to become coach at the Racquet Club of Philadelphia. Soutar was world champion of the older game of rackets for 16 years, from 1913-1929. His build *'with the chest and shoulders of a young Hercules'* and his hard hitting style also suited squash, in the American hardball version. In 1914 he won a series of squash matches against Canadian pros, proving him the best in North America. He won the first Professional squash championship of America in 1916, defended this title successfully in 1920, and held it until 1925, when he retired undefeated in American squash.

Canada

Canada meanwhile was only five years behind, their first national champion being Kenneth Molson in 1912, in an all-Montreal player final played at the Montreal Racket Club. This, three years before the 1915 formation of the Canadian Association.

The Association takes charge, sort of, maybe

The Tennis & Rackets Association was founded in England in 1907, to govern the ancient games of real tennis and rackets. Afterwards fives was included in the name too. Because squash, the off-spring game, was rapidly becoming popular, a sub-committee for squash was added in 1908, its first task to draw up a set of rules. A year later their proposal for a 'standard' squash

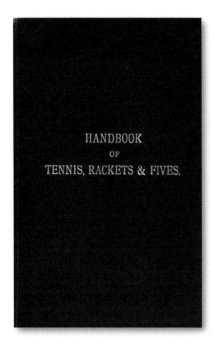

court was accepted, and the new rules were published in the Association's handbook in 1912. Barely two pages, they were a bit vague, to say the least. They mentioned a 'standard court' of 30 x 21 feet, but at the same time stated that in no case the length should be more than 36 feet or less than 26. They even suggested several other court sizes that would *'…be practically as good as the standard size.'* So much for uniformity! As for the playing rules they printed: *'There are no separate rules for squash rackets. The common practice is that the rules of rackets shall be in force in so far as they apply.'* Not very instructive either. It was not until the 1920s, that the T&RA finally laid down firm standard rules, no doubt to the relief of all squash referees.

Chase the ace

You can win a point with an ace in tennis, but in squash an ace was a point! When the squash rules were printed by the Tennis Rackets & Fives Association in 1912, a point was called an ace. These aces/points could only be won by the server: the hand-in, hand-out system. To win the match two games had to be won. Games were up to 15 points rather than up to nine which came into being only later, when the rules were further standardised.

Weigall's way

Another populariser of squash was 'Gerry' (G.J.V.) Weigall. His background was similar to many of the early players: coming from a wealthy family, and with a public school and university (Cambridge) education under his belt. Born in 1870 he became an excellent squash player. He frequently wrote articles to promote the game, including this early coaching manual, 16 pages long, which also deals with the building of courts. Weigall was an active administrator too and helped revise the rules as squash representative on the Tennis & Rackets Association. Even in his fifties he was still playing squash for Lord's MCC at high amateur level.

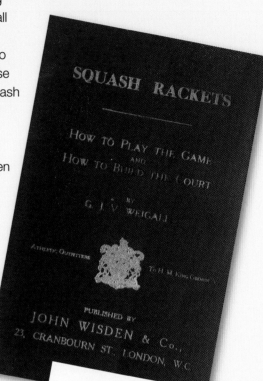

▶ Some images from Weigall's booklet. Published about 1913, it was only the second ever book on squash.

Exterior

Interior by Night.

Illustrations of a Modern Squash Racket Court.

▲ Weigall demonstrating the correct positions for the backhand stroke.

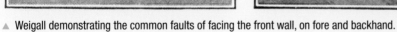

▲ Weigall demonstrating the common faults of facing the front wall, on fore and backhand.

▲ Equipment in Weigall's day.

The first court directory

This booklet was published in 1913 by the squash sub-committee of the Tennis Rackets & Fives Association, and was an attempt to register all the known squash courts in Great Britain. There were 170 squash courts in total in the UK at that point, not even including the public school courts. The majority on the list were privately owned courts like the one at Knowle Hall in Knowle, Warwickshire.

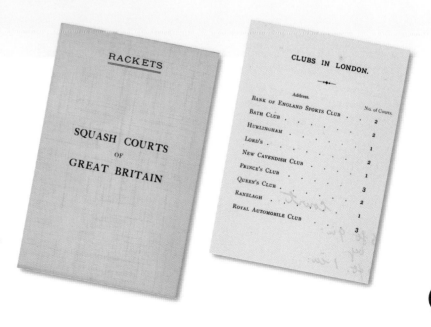

Selling squash

T. H. Prosser & Sons was founded in 1857 as maker of equipment for the older game of rackets. Soon they started producing equipment for all popular sports. During the 19th century they were the official supplier to Harrow School of rackets rackets, and in this position they must have been (one of) the first firm(s) who started producing equipment specifically for squash. By 1893 Prosser were already advertising their squash balls. In the first ever book about the game in 1901, Prosser is recommended for squash equipment. These images of their London factory at Holloway Road come from a book of photographs (c1907).

N° 1 SECTION OF LAWN TENNIS, BADMINTON SQUASH & RACQUET MAKING DEPT.

N° 1 SECTION STOCK ROOM FOR FINISHED GOODS

The Titanic

The Titanic, the largest passenger steamship of the time, had a squash court. It was available for first class passengers, who could take lessons from Fred Wright. He had previously worked

as squash coach at the Bath Club in London, before being hired by the Cunard Line: first on the Olympic (1911) which also had a squash court, and then on its new sister ship, the Titanic. Wright was one of the over 1,500 who perished when it went down on its maiden trip in 1912.

Australia

Australia was relatively late to introduce squash. The country's first squash courts are believed to have been built in 1913 at the Melbourne Club (photo). Still existing today, it was and is an exclusive male only social club, founded in 1838, and located in Collins Street. Here in 1913 the club's former large indoor rackets court (which had been built in 1876) was converted into two squash courts, although both not yet standard size. Other early Australian squash courts were found in Gostwyck (Uralla, NSW) where in December 1912 captain C.C. Dangar hired a contractor to build a private court at his estate. And in Sydney in September 1914 the Bjelke-Petersen New Physical Culture School opened at 68 Elizabeth St., including a squash court, open to 'all and sundry', a very early example of a public court!

The Netherlands

After learning the game while staying in London, the Dutch Count Bentinck then built the first squash court in the Netherlands at his Middachten Castle in 1914. The enclosed court with its cement floor and its attractive wooden roof structure has recently been restored and is in play again today.

CHAPTER 3

SQUASH IN THE 1920s

By the early twenties squash administration had restarted after the end of World War 1. The beginning of the London team competition for the Bath Cup lead to standardisation, and the court size was laid down. British championships started for amateurs and for professionals, with Charles Read dominating the decade. For women, the British Open began with the Cave sisters often victorious. International matches were initiated, and the (British) Squash Rackets Association was founded.

SQUASH IN THE 1920s
Setting standards

A key moment for squash was the start of the Bath Club Cup in 1922; a squash league between the various London clubs. For the first time there were regular matches between their best (amateur) players. An instant success, it also demonstrated the urgent need for standardisation: players in this new competition found they had to play on six different sized courts and with five different ball types!

In 1923 the Tennis and Rackets Association appointed a new, enlarged sub-committee to look after squash and its standardisation. It consisted of delegates from various clubs, meetings being held at the RAC. In 1923 they laid down the standard size of a squash court, at 32 x 21 feet (9.75 x 6.40 metres), based on the size of the court in use at the Bath Club. The tin height was set at 19 inches (48cm). For squash throughout the world (with the exception of North America) there was clarity at last, and this court size is still the standard today.

Next up was the selection of a standard ball, of optimum size and speed. In 1923 the committee first considered the existing four most popular ball types: the Wisden Royal, the Gradidge ball, the RAC ball, and the Bath Club holer. More tests were carried out, and in 1926 they introduced a new mark, 'TRA standard' that only their new approved balls were allowed to carry. In the following years the standard would be changed several more times, the ball gradually becoming slower, but at least there now was one standard for match playing, a huge step forward.

The scoring system was also changed. Until 1926 games had been up to 15 points (like its parent sport rackets), winner best of three games. But from 1926, games would be to 9 points, and winner best of five games. With all these changes, in a time span of only a few years, this T&RA sub-committee laid the foundations of squash for years to come.

▲ The Tennis and Rackets Association was responsible for British squash before 1928 when a separate squash association was formed. The T&RA awarded these bronze medals (showing the rackets for the three sports) to the runners up in the Amateur squash championship.

1928-1929.

TENNIS AND RACKETS ASSOCIATION.
Squash Rackets Sub-Committee.

THE BATH CLUB CUP.

Inter - Club Squash
Rackets Tournament

The "Sports Trader" Series.

RACKETS
and
SQUASH
LAWS

As approved by the
Tennis, Rackets & Fives Association

W. H. SMITH & SON
1 0 0 0   B R A N C H E S
Head Office : Strand House,
Portugal St., London, W.C.2.

▲ Rules booklet dating from about 1920, when squash was not yet firmly standardised.

WISDEN

Royal Craftsmen of Sport since 1850.

The Super Squash Racket.

Authorised by the Tennis & Rackets Asscn. Adopted for the Amateur Chamionships.

SOLD BY ALL SPORTS OUTFITTERS

JOHN WISDEN & CO., LIMITED.

▲ Wisden advertisement (1929) showing the T&RA approved squash ball mark.

▲ Early squash courts differed in size, such as at Queen's (top) or the Bath Club (bottom). The Bath Club's court served as a model for the new standard court size introduced in 1926.

Club balls

Gradidge squash ball (3.8 cm diameter). This model was one of the most widely used balls during the early 20th century and was especially popular at the London Queen's Club. Produced from c1900-c1930 (version shown dating from pre1926) the ball was available in three colours: white, black and red.

Together with an RAC Number two ball (4.0 cm), with high gloss black enamelled surface, and the club's logo. It was developed in 1924 in the search for a new slower standard ball, as an alternative for the popular original RAC ball. Production ceased soon after 1926, when the standard was changed yet again.

A royal racket

The Prince of Wales, the future King Edward VIII, was a keen player at the Bath Club, where he was coached by Charles Arnold. 'The most popular man in the British Empire', his exploits on the squash court received a lot of press coverage and he even entered the Amateur and Army championships.

For touring the dominions during the 1920s, battlecruisers like the HMS Renown had been refitted as his royal yacht, including a squash court on board. Although he regularly showed up late for official functions because he preferred to play squash, his playing did help raise interest in squash in the countries he visited, like Australia and Canada.

◀ Silver mounted squash racket, presented to the Prince of Wales, as runner up in the prestigious Bath Club handicap tournament in 1920.

THE BATH CLUB – SQUASH RACQUET HANDICAP
SECOND PRIZE WON BY H.R.H. THE PRINCE OF WALES K.G.
2ND MARCH 1920

▲ The Prince supported this book (1926) by Charles Arnold, his coach at the Bath Club.

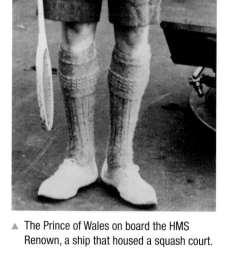

▲ The Prince of Wales on board the HMS Renown, a ship that housed a squash court.

Nancy Cave (left) and Eileen Nicholson, who met at the Women's championship in November 1922.

Ladies leading

The Women's championship was first held in February 1922, even before the men started theirs. Until WW2 the championship was played at the Queen's Club in London. It would later be called the British Open and was regarded as the de-facto World championship. At the start in 1922 the first round was played in round robin groups. But since 1928 the tournament has been played in the straight knock out format. During the 1920s, all finals were contested between only four women.

The first winner in February 1922 was 19 year old Joyce Cave. She would win the title three times (in 1922/24/28), being runner up on three more occasions. Joyce was known for her strong backhand, that was even better than her forehand. She played squash (usually doubles) with her sisters and brothers at the large court attached to their family home. They had been taught by their father, who as a boy represented Rugby at rackets. Her sister Nancy Cave, six years her senior, was a stylish player who hit the ball hard and low (in the rackets tradition). She competed in the championship nine times, reaching the final on each occasion and winning three of them (in 1923/29/30), which makes her the most succesful female player of the 1920s.

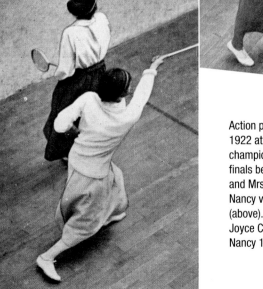

Action photos from February 1922 at the first Women's championship. The semi-finals between Joyce Cave and Mrs Bruce (left) and Nancy vs Marjorie Cave (above). In the final (top) Joyce Cave beat her sister Nancy 11-15, 15-10, 15-9.

Sylvia Huntsman surprisingly won the Women's championship in November 1922, her only appearance in the final. She was not in the same class as the Caves, but as one reporter put it *'one always likes to see her determination'*.

Cicely Fenwick won the Women's championship three times (1925/26/31). She had a court of her own in Gloucestershire, and received coaching from Charles Read. Her technique was less refined than that of the Caves, but Fenwick was known for her *'great powers of return'*. She played *'grim and intensive squash'*, and it was reported that she *'kills the easy ball from the middle of the court very severely indeed for a lady player'*.

Sylvia Huntsman

▲ In the first Women's championship in 1922 three of the four semi finalists were sisters! From left to right: Joyce, Marjorie and Nancy Cave.

▲ Joyce Cave

▲ Cicely Fenwick

Peerage at play

The women who played squash during this era were very much from the upper classes: when a 1922 sports magazine wrote about the best female players in England, it listed one Marchioness, one Viscountess, three Ladies and one Honourable Mrs., of a total of only 22 women mentioned!

Pros progress

The 'Three Musketeers', the club pros who together dominated squash during the 1910s & 20s: Oak Johnson, Charles Read and Charles Arnold (from left to right). They are pictured here in 1949, at the 21st anniversary of the Squash Rackets Association.

The three played a crucial role in the popularisation of squash and its development into a serious sport.

Arnold at the Bath

Charles Arnold was the professional at the London Bath Club, where he started c1911 and soon succeeded G. Bannister as head pro. Before that he had been a champion roller skater and boxer. Arnold coached many successful amateur players, including Victor Cazalet, but is best known for coaching the Prince of Wales (the future King Edward VIII). In 1931 Arnold, 47 years old, challenged the much younger Donald Butcher, the title holder, for the combined British Open and Professional championship, but was badly beaten. Arnold worked at the Bath Club for over 25 years, and also had his own squash racket brand and court construction company.

▲ Squash racket (c1920-25) with cord bound shoulders and two tone stringing, marked 'C. Arnold (professional) Bath Club London'.

15. 12. 31

Johnson's 45 years

Oak (A.W.B.) Johnson was pro at the RAC clubhouse in London from its opening in 1911 until his death in 1956. Originally hired as coach for the intended real tennis court, building plans changed and Johnson found himself in charge of three squash courts instead! Johnson quickly became one of the top three squash players in the country. In 1920 and 1928 he played Charles Read for the British Professional championship but lost. Oak (also called Oke) is best remembered as coach of the legendary Amr Bey, who referred to him as *'my friend and tutor'*. From 1928, in less than three years, Johnson turned the Egyptian, who had just taken up the game, into an unbeatable champion.

▲ Coach Johnson at the Royal Automobile Club at Pall Mall, London, (c1920). Members were charged 1s for half an hour on court with him.

▶ A present to his coach Oak Johnson, a silver match box, hallmarked 1928, gilded interior engraved *'from Amr Bey'*.

Read reigns

Charles Read (1889-1962) started as ball boy aged 13 at the Queen's Club in London, before going to Harrow to assist his uncle 'Judy' Stevens, the school's rackets professional. When he was 17, Read returned to Queen's as head pro and worked there for over 30 years. He taught squash, rackets and lawn tennis; and would become champion of all three sports. In squash he played his first professional match when he beat G. Bannister, the Bath Club pro, apparently in 1907; a win he repeated in 1913. Read confirmed he was the undisputed champion by decisively beating Jimmy Palmer-Tomkinson, the leading amateur squash player, around the same time.

Professional champion

Competitive play was still limited in those early days, but Read would remain unbeaten until 1930, a period of more than 20 years! Stockily built, he posessed *'certainty of return and great control of placing the ball … No amount of running tires him'*. He was challenged for the newly instituted British Professional squash championship (a home and away match for GB£200) in 1920, and again in 1928, by Oak Johnson, whom he beat easily on each occasion. When the British Open was first held in 1930, the Association designated Read as champion. But by then he was already 41 years old and had just recovered from illness. Read lost to Donald Butcher, his 25 year old challenger; the end of a great champion's reign.

◀ Charles Read was the only player ever to simultaneously hold the British Professional championship of squash (1920-1930), and also of rackets (1925-1932) and of lawn tennis (1920-1923 and 1925-1928); for the third he was awarded this silver trophy.

▲ Slazenger advertisement (1927) for the Read squash racket.

▲ Charles Read demonstrating a forehand half-volley for the game of rackets in a cinematography sequence (1926).

Amateurs all in

In April 1923 the British men held their first Amateur championship. Played in London, the first edition was held at Lord's, after that it was hosted by the Bath Club. In those days playing a sport was considered to be just one of many diverse upper class activities. So if he excelled at a sport, the amateur was to be admired even more than the pro whose paid job it was. Newspapers published daily reports about each round of the Amateur championship, back then possibly the squash tournament with the strongest entry in the world.

The very best of all amateurs was Jimmy Palmer-Tomkinson. A member of the Bath Club, from its opening in 1904 for nearly twenty years he was virtually unbeatable. He, the Charles Read among amateurs, even once challenged Read himself, but lost. In the Bath Club handicap competitions Tomkinson gave collossal odds, but still won. He was a stylish player, known for his changes of pace and angles. But a war injury hindered his play. He lost three of the first four Amateur finals, before eventually lifting the trophy in December 1926, a 'most popular victory', at the age of 47!

The first two championships had been won by Tommy Jameson, a tall Irish born player, who hit hard up and down the wall in the Harrow rackets style, and had 'an enormous reach, great speed and a wonderful eye'. But ill health soon forced him out of the game.

CAPT. J. PALMER-TOMKINSON

▲ Jimmy Palmer-Tomkinson was the dominant British amateur player for nearly twenty years. Also an active administrator, he became chairman and later president of the SRA.

▲ The finalists of the Amateur championship in December 1923, the second time it was held. Title holder Tommy Jameson (left) beat Cecil Browning (right).

Dugald Macpherson, a beautiful stylist with 'exquisite footwork and delicacy of stroke' also took the title twice (1924/28). His touch contrasted greatly with Victor Cazalet, the decade's most successful amateur, who reached six successive finals, winning four (1926Jan/27/29/30). Not a subtle player but 'his great fighting spirit and powers of return' made him a feared opponent.

New competitions

In the 1920s, for men in Britain there were many other annual squash championships instituted, including for the Army (1925), the Oxford and Cambridge intervarsity (c1925), the Interservices (c1928) and the Inter County (1929). For boys the Public Schools Handicap contest was started, for which this silver trophy was awarded in 1926 to Charles Wilson from Repton School. The talented Wilson would also win the first two editions of the 'Drysdale Cup' tournament. It was named after Theodore Drysdale, a leading amateur player, member of the first British team and active administrator, who wanted to encourage junior squash. Still played today and known as the British Junior Open for Boys Under 19, it started at the RAC in London in 1926.

Amateur championship winners Victor Cazalet (4x champion) and Dugald Macpherson (left, 2x champion) during a match in 1931.

▶ Medal awarded to 'Ginger' Basset, the runner up in the 1929 Amateur championship who played for the RAC and was another early squash administrator.

▲ Sam Toyne, the veteran player, semi finalist in the first Amateur championship in 1923. He was captain of the first ever British squash team in 1924.

The Amateur championship final in 1929, between Cazalet (right) and Basset.

The American cousins

In North America the hardball variant was played. The difference with English/international squash further increased in 1920 when the American court width was standardised at 18 1/2 foot, and two years later the tin height, at 17 inch (so narrower and with a lower tin than what would become the standard internationally). The Canadian Association affiliated with the Americans in 1921 and followed their standards. New annual competitions were instituted in the US, such as the Harvard-Yale intercollegiate contest (1923) and the US Women's National championship (1928). A key moment was when Harvard in 1921 hired Harry Cowles as coach for the college squash team. In no time he made Harvard the dominant factor in American squash: during Cowles' employment there, Harvard men won 13 out of 16 straight US National Singles championships!

▲ Harry Cowles, successful Harvard coach, portrait decal on a squash racket (c1930) from his sports shop.

▲ Herbert Rawlins, twice US National champion (1928 & 30) had learned squash from coach Cowles at Harvard.

◄ Eleonora Sears, winner of the first American women's national championship in 1928.

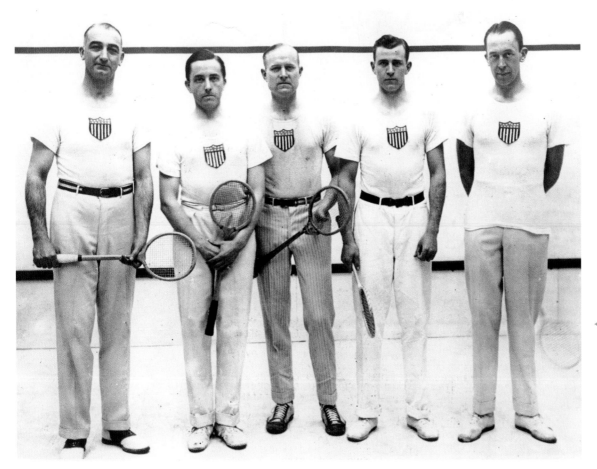

◄ In 1925, the USA squash team was sent overseas but was heavily defeated by the British. From left to right: A. Edward Ells, Joseph de V. Keefe, Henry Mills, Eugene Hinkle and C. Sewall Clark.

▲ Gold medals awarded to George Debevoise in 1924 & 25, for the Harvard singles championship, and for winning the Massachusetts Inter-club competition with his Harvard team.

▶ Three American squash rackets (c1920s) with experimental designs: a Wright & Ditson Top Flite with open throat, a Harry C Lee racket with raised shoulder parts, and a metal and wood racket with its unusual steel wire strings by the Dayton Steel Racquet Company from Ohio. The American hardball variant used heavier and sturdier frames compared with English squash rackets.

Founding of the Squash Rackets Association

During the 1920s squash administration continued to be handled by a sub-committee of the Tennis and Rackets Association. However squash was becoming increasingly popular and started to get in the way of real tennis and rackets, the Association's core activities. And so the former sub-committee officially became the Squash Rackets Association (SRA), founded in December 1928. Although for the first few years the SRA was still affiliated with the T&RA, from its founding it ran British squash independently. Headquarters of the SRA were at the Royal Automobile Club in London, with the club's secretary, Mr Peasgood, in charge of SRA administration. Lord Wodehouse became chairman and the celebrated player Palmer-Tomkinson, vice-chairman. Other national squash associations and overseas clubs soon affiliated with the SRA, which acted as the de facto world wide squash governing body.

▶ The Royal Automobile Club at Pall Mall in London, from 1928 onwards the headquarters of the newly founded SRA.

▲ The British returned to North America in 1927, winning the Lapham team cup and the Canadian singles championship (won by Cazalet). The team consisted of: William 'Ginger' Basset (1st on the right), Victor Cazalet (2nd right), Philip de L. Cazenove, Harry Coverdale, Godfrey Incledon-Webber, George Scott-Chad (2nd left), Frank Strawson (3rd left).

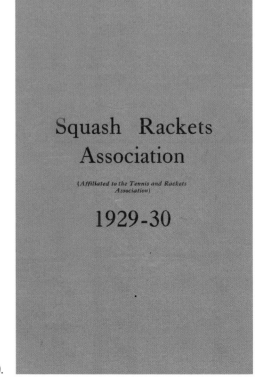

Squash Rackets Association

(Affiliated to the Tennis and Rackets Association)

1929-30

▶ The first SRA handbook was published in 1929.

Internationals

International squash started in 1922 for men when the annual Lapham Cup contest between the USA and Canada was held for the first time. It was not until 1929 that Canada scored its first win. The Cup is still played for each year by these two countries. Trans-Atlantic squash began in 1924, when the British team toured North America, the first time a national team travelled overseas. Gerald 'Timmy' Robarts, the 46 year old from England, remained unbeaten, winning 17 matches in 19 days, including the American and Canadian singles championship; an indication of the difference in strength, despite the Americans' home advantage of the hardball game. This was all the more apparent when the USA team went to England the following year, and again in 1928 and were badly beaten.

▲ No dinners in tracksuits in those days! The British and American teams at the London Bath Club in 1925.

Back row, left to right: Sir John Wilson Taylor, Gerald Robarts (GB), A. Edward Ells (USA), William 'Ginger' Basset (GB), Victor Cazalet (GB), Lord Wodehouse.

Sitting: Henry Mills (USA), Dugald Macpherson (GB), Eugene Hinkle (USA), Lord Desborough, Jimmy Palmer-Tomkinson (GB), C. Sewall Clark (USA), Joseph de V. Keefe (USA).

▲ Victor Cazalet with Henri de Sibour (left), the Washington team captain, during the British team tour in 1927.

Courts around the world

In South America squash made some new entries in the 1920s. In Brazil, British employees of a mining company in Nova Lima had a court built at the Clube das Quintas. In Argentina, 'The Squash Club', launched by a British group on Florida Street in Buenos Aires in 1929, is still active.

In Hong Kong two rackets courts at the Victoria Barracks were converted into six squash courts, evidently during the 1920s. The site was later used for building the Hong Kong Squash Centre (pictured), that opened in 1986 and has 18 courts on three levels. There are now over 500 courts in Hong Kong.

In Australia at the Royal Melbourne Tennis Club in 1928, club pro Woolner Stone won the final of the first Australian squash championship, beating Captain G.A. 'Bo' Fairbairn, who had donated the perpetual trophy. From 1929 pros could no longer enter and it became the Australian Amateur championship.

In France there's mention of squash in Pau in 1901, and courts built by British soldiers during WW1 (1914-18). But the real start was in Paris in 1927 when the Société Sportive du Jeu de Paume turned one of the club's real tennis courts into four small squash courts.

CHAPTER 4

SQUASH IN THE 1930s

Squash was starting to become more popular, new courts being built throughout the UK, but it was still an elite sport. The men's British Open was instituted, soon dominated by an Egyptian amateur, Amr Bey, who beat all the British professionals. Women's squash was raised to new levels by Margot Lumb. Many other countries began holding national championships. Women's federations were formed and the first international women's matches were played.

Donald Butcher with the British
Professional championship trophy.

Butcher's big win

From its start the British Open was the most prestigious squash tournament in the world, and it remained so for many decades. Before 1948 it was held as a home and away challenge contest. It was first played in December 1930; in those days for a purse of GB£100, the winner taking 2/3. The challenger was Donald Butcher, a 25-year old London pro; his opponent Charles Read, who as the reigning British Professional champion had been designated Open title holder. The legendary Read had not lost a match on his home court at Queen's for 25 years, and the betting was 100 to 8 in his favour. But Read was already 41 years old, and illness had hindered his preparation. Butcher won at Queen's 9-6 9-5 9-5 and at his own Conservative Club 9-3 9-5 9-3, each leg lasting nearly 60 minutes.

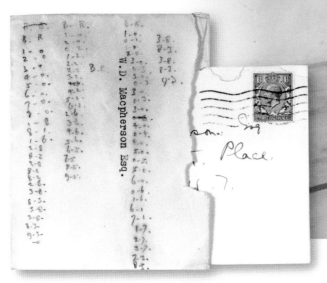

▲ For the first British Open in 1930, marker Dugald Macpherson used the back of an envelope.

First doping case?

In February 1938 an out of shape Donald Butcher took two tablets before stepping on court to beat the much younger squash pro Jack Aylott. After their 45-minute match Butcher reported that he had *'never felt better... The ball looked as big as a football'*. Aylott had not known of Butcher's intake, which led to a row and even an official enquiry. All ended well once it was explained that Butcher had taken the tablets as an experiment at the request of a doctor friend. Their contents? Benzedrine, better known as amphetamine.

Two titles

Butcher was a stylist with a very sound technique. He practiced his accuracy by aiming at a penny placed on top of the tin. His victory made him the new holder of both the British Professional and the British Open title. In 1931 Butcher defended these with ease against Charles Arnold, another veteran pro from Read's era. The next year Butcher lost his British Open title to Amr Bey, an amateur; but he held his Professional title until 1935, when he lost to Jim Dear, who had tried to win it from him two years earlier.

The D. G. BUTCHER
Squash Rackets

Made by Hand from the finest materials obtainable
THE
D. G. Butcher
Super Model
25/-

Butcher Autograph Model 21/-

OBTAINABLE from all leading Sports Dealers, including Lilly-whites, Army and Navy Stores, Selfridges, Harrods, Marshall and Snelgrove, etc., etc.

SOLE MANUFACTURERS :
BOYS, O'BRIEN & Co., Ltd.
8 Smith's Court, Great Windmill Street, W.1

▲ Advertisement for Butcher's signature racket (1937).

Egyptian class

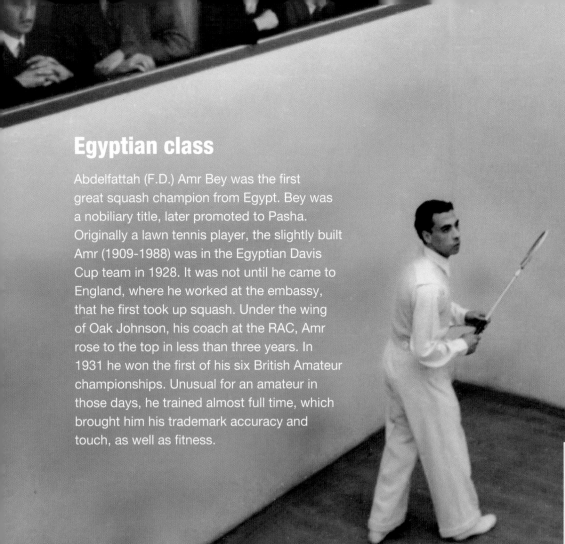

Abdelfattah (F.D.) Amr Bey was the first great squash champion from Egypt. Bey was a nobiliary title, later promoted to Pasha. Originally a lawn tennis player, the slightly built Amr (1909-1988) was in the Egyptian Davis Cup team in 1928. It was not until he came to England, where he worked at the embassy, that he first took up squash. Under the wing of Oak Johnson, his coach at the RAC, Amr rose to the top in less than three years. In 1931 he won the first of his six British Amateur championships. Unusual for an amateur in those days, he trained almost full time, which brought him his trademark accuracy and touch, as well as fitness.

Amr in action at the Bath Club.

▶ Amr on the cover of a 1936 magazine.

Open champion

Amr Bey challenged professional Donald Butcher, the title holder, for the British Open in 1932. The first leg at Butcher's Conservative Club was won by Amr 9-0 9-7 9-1. In the return at the Bath Club he won again 5-9 5-9 9-2 9-1 9-0. Amr was equal to Butcher in stroke play, but much fitter and *'as light on his feet as a ballet dancer and as fast about the court as quicksilver'.* In very few sports at the time was an amateur better than all professionals. This, combined with Amr's *'old-world courtesy'* and being of Egyptian blue blood ensured a lot of publicity for squash. He would hold the British Open title for six years, beating professionals Donald Butcher two times (1932/34) and the younger Jim Dear three times (1935/36/37); in 1933 no match was held. Amr retired in 1938 as undefeated British Open champion, to pursue his diplomatic career, becoming Egyptian ambassador in 1945.

▲ Silver medal presented to Amr by the SRA in 1933.

▲ Signed dinner menu on the occasion of the England v USA match in 1935. The Egyptian Amr had, uniquely, been asked to play for the English team as captain.

▲ Action shots taken at the 1936 British Open between Dear (left) and Amr.

No let

In the two matches for the 1935 British Open between Amr Bey and Dear *'not a single let'* occurred. Amr was *'one of the fairest of players'*, and often made way for his opponents to his own disadvantage. In those days, it was considered bad form to cause a let: *'For be it remembered it is always slightly ignominious for the loser to be obliged to ask for lets'*.

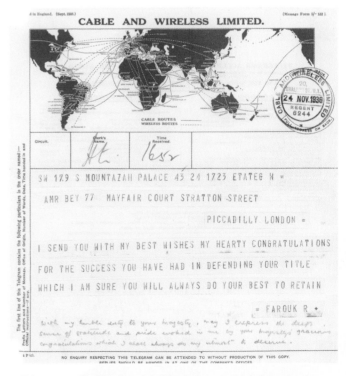

▲ Telegram sent by King Farouk I of Egypt to congratulate Amr when he won the 1936 British Open.

Amateurs second best

Amr Bey won six British Amateur championships between 1931 and 1937, beating an Englishman in each final. His strongest opponent was former champion Dugald Macpherson (1931). Edward Snell, a schoolmaster, was runner up three times (1932/35/36). Snell was known for his lobbing game which caused problems for all, except Amr. Other finalists easily disposed of were Capt. Guy Jameson, a retriever (1933); and John Stokes, a stroke player (1937). In 1934 both Amr and Snell were absent, when Cyril Hamilton, another army man, won the tournament.

Master of the unorthodox

One of the few that could trouble Amr Bey was the tall Kenneth Gandar-Dower. 'The Gandar', aka 'Kangaroo' or 'Iconoclast' became Amateur champion in 1938 after Amr had retired. He had a unique if ungainly style: always facing the front wall, taking balls half-volley, often finding the nick; and all this combined with staying power. He held the record for representing Cambridge University at seven sports (including squash) and he was unorthodox at all of them. An aviator, journalist, adventurer and eccentric, he once walked his favorite cheetah Pongo into the bar of the Queen's Club.

Gandar-Dower with Pongo

▲ Snell forced to play a backwall boast against Amr. Snell lost three British Amateur finals but did win the Canadian (hardball) championship in 1934.

▲ Amr congratulated after winning his sixth Amateur title.

▶ The 1937 Amateur final - Bath Club's main (back wall) galleries.

THE MEN WHO HAVE BECOME SQUASH'S BRITISH OPEN CHAMPIONS

WORLD SQUASH LIBRARY

CHARLES READ (ENG)
[1] 1930 (designated)

DONALD BUTCHER (ENG)
[2] 1930,31

F D AMR BEY (EGY)
[5] 1932,4,5,6,7

JIM DEAR (ENG)
[1] 1938

MAHMOUD KARIM (EGY)
[4] 1947, 8, 9, 50

HASHIM KHAN (PAK)
[7] 1951,2,3,4,5,6,8

ROSHAN KHAN (PAK)
[1] 1957

AZAM KHAN (PAK)
[4] 1959(2),60,1

MOHIBULLAH KHAN (PAK)
[1] 1962

ABDELFATTAH ABOUTALEB (EGY)
[3] 1963,4,5

JONAH BARRINGTON (IRL)
[6] 1966,7, 9,70,2,3

GEOFF HUNT (AUS)
[8] 1969,74,6,7,8,9,80,1

QAMAR ZAMAN (PAK)
[1] 1975

JAHANGIR KHAN (PAK)
[10] 1982,3,4,5,6,7,8,9,90,1

JANSHER KHAN (PAK)
[6] 1992,3,4,5,6,7

PETER NICOL (SCO/ENG)
[2] 1998,02

JONATHON POWER (CAN)
[1] 1999

DAVID EVANS (WAL)
[1] 2000

DAVID PALMER (AUS)
[4] 2001,3,4,8

ANTHONY RICKETTS (AUS)
[1] 2005

NICK MATTHEW (ENG)
[3] 2006,9,12

GREGORY GAULTIER (FRA)
[3] 2007,14,17

RAMY ASHOUR (EGY)
[1] 2013

MOHAMED ELSHORBAGY (EGY)
[3] 2015,16,19

MIGUEL A RODRIGUEZ (COL)
[1] 2018

PAUL COLL (NZL)
[2] 2021,22

ALI FARAG (EGY)
[1] 2023

MOSTAFA ASAL (EGY)
[1] 2024

For British Open results;
www.squashinfo.com
www.squashlibrary.info
info@squashlibrary.info

Squash archive and
information resource

*Many photos kindly
supplied by Steve Line*

Squash Info

WORLD SQUASH LIBRARY
THE SQUASH RESULTS
& ARCHIVE HUBS

Susan Noel holding the trophy of the US championship she won in 1933.

Susan's success

Susan Noel was, as she described it, *'practically born with a racket in her hand'*. She grew up near the Queen's Club in London where her father Evan B. Noel was the Club secretary. He belonged to an aristocratic family and had been Olympic rackets champion in 1908. At Queen's he initiated the Women's squash championship (later called the British Open). She competed in the tournament from age 12, and was still only 19 when she first won in 1932, beating former champion Joyce Cave in the final. Noel also took the next two titles, winning the last final 9-7 9-0 9-6 against Margot Lumb, who would become her successor. Noel was the first woman who won the championship three times in a row.

Noel raised the standard of women's squash with her attacking play and use of drops and angles. In 1933 & 34 she led the British women's team that won the first two international contests against the USA. On tour with the British, Noel also won the US singles (hardball) championship. She retired in 1934 to focus on her lawn tennis but made a brief comeback five years later. There had been a debate in newspapers about who was the best of all female squash players, Noel or her successor Margot Lumb. The two met again in the final of the 1939 Women's championship, but this time Noel lost.

▶ Noel wrote frequently about squash and published two books on the game.

Noel (bottom) playing Margot Lumb in the 1939 Women's championship final.

◀ Silver trophy awarded to Noel in 1939 for winning the South of England tournament; after the Women's championship the most prestigious in the UK.

▲ Cartoon from an American newspaper when Noel was touring the US in 1933.

▲ The first British women's squash team arriving in New York on board the S.S. Aquitania in 1933. Left to right: Hon. Anne Lytton-Milbanke, Susan Noel, Betty Daniell, Cicely Fenwick, Eliza Bryans Wolfe (captain), Nancy Cave, Gwenda du Boulay.

▲ The US team traveling to the UK in 1934 for the second international women's match, which they would lose 0-5. Left to right: Anne Page (US champion 1936/37/39/47), Adelaide Stuart Green, Agnes Lamme, Marguerite Anderson, Margaret Howe (US champion 1929/32/34), Cecile 'Babe' Bowes (US champion 1938/40/41/48). Not depicted is Eleonora Sears (team captain).

Women go international

The first international women's match took place in February 1933 at the Sleepy Hollow Country Club, N.Y. where the visiting Great Britain team beat their hosts USA 4-1. After the event British team members Eliza Bryans Wolfe (pictured left) and Susan Noel donated a silver trophy for the match to be held alternating between the two nations, the Wolfe-Noel Cup, at first every year but biennially after 1937. International women's squash was born.

The men initiated new international matches too. The first contest between the UK home countries was in 1938 when England beat Scotland 6-1. Scotland also first played Ireland that year, winning 4-1. In Europe mainland, Sweden against Denmark is believed to have already been held once shortly before the war.

THE WOMEN WHO HAVE BECOME SQUASH'S BRITISH OPEN CHAMPIONS

WSL

WORLD SQUASH LIBRARY

JOYCE CAVE (ENG)
[3] 1922,4,8

SYLVIA HUNTSMAN (ENG)
[1] 1922

NANCY CAVE (ENG)
[3] 1923,9,30

CICELY FENWICK (ENG)
[3] 1925,6,31

SUSAN NOEL (ENG)
[3] 1932,3,4

MARGOT LUMB (ENG)
[5] 1934,6,7,8,9

JOAN CURRY (ENG)
[3] 1947,8,9

JANET MORGAN (ENG)
[10] 1950,1(2),3,4(2),6,7,8(2)

SHEILA MACINTOSH (ENG)
[1] 1960

FRAN MARSHALL (ENG)
[1] 1961

HEATHER McKAY (AUS)
[16] 1962(2),4,5,6,7,8,9,70,1,2,3,4,5,
6,7 (nee Blundell 62-5)

SUE NEWMAN (AUS)
[1] 1978

BARBARA WALL (AUS)
[1] 1979

VICKI CARDWELL (AUS)
[4] 1980,1,2,3 (nee Hoffman 80-1)

SUSAN DEVOY (NZL)
[8] 1984,5,6,7,8,9,90,2

LISA OPIE (ENG)
[1] 1991

MICHELLE MARTIN (AUS)
[6] 1993,4,5,6,7,8

LEILANI JOYCE (NZL)
[2] 1999,00

SARAH FITZ-GERALD (AUS)
[2] 2001,2

RACHAEL GRINHAM (AUS)
[4] 2003,4,7,9

NICOL DAVID (MAS)
[5] 2005,6,8,12,14

LAURA MASSARO (ENG)
[2] 2013,17

CAMILLE SERME (FRA)
[1] 2015

NOUR EL SHERBINI (EGY)
[4] 2016, 18, 21, 23

NOURAN GOHAR (EGY)
[2] 2019,24

HANIA EL HAMMAMY (EGY)
[1] 2022

For British Open results;
www.squashinfo.com
www.squashlibrary.info
info@squashlibrary.info

Squash archive and
information resource

Many photos kindly supplied by Steve Line

Squash **Info**

WORLD SQUASH LIBRARY

THE SQUASH RESULTS
& ARCHIVE HUBS

Squash mechanics

In the 1930s US scientists were beginning to experiment with stroboscopic lighting to capture movement on photo. This 1938 image shows Jack Summers, four-time US Professional champion, hitting a squash ball with his forehand. This was the first time that the mechanics of the squash stroke became visible to the human eye.

DEPENDABILITY
CONSISTENCY
DURABILITY

...the choice of
all keen players

▲ By the mid-1930s approved balls, such as this Silvertown one, carried the stamp of the Squash Rackets Association.

Solid Wood

College racket by Wisden still made in the traditional way of a single piece of steam bent wood (c1930). Around that time a new stronger type of squash racket, laminated by glueing strips of wood together, was already on its way to becoming popular, and it would not be long before the production of solid wooden rackets ceased.

Court construction

A British newspaper observed in 1937 that *'squash is spreading with the rapidity of an epidemic'*. There was a great demand for the building of new courts, and several specialised firms seized the opportunity. One such firm was Bickley, who already had a long tradition in rackets courts; another was Carter's, whose squash courts, whether brick or timber, were the most popular both in the UK and across mainland Europe. Carter's also built a few doubles courts, like at the St. John's Wood Club in London (pic).

Squash in print

Squash was already starting to get more coverage in newspapers and magazines when two new British publications appeared for the first time. In October 1932 'Squash Rackets, Fives, Tennis and Rackets', the first magazine with a specific focus on squash, was launched; followed in 1936/37 by the 'Squash Rackets Annual', in book form. Both ran until the outbreak of war in 1939.

Dear's triple

Jim Dear was a natural with the racket. At the Queen's Club during slow hours, while his fellow ball boys were practising, young Jimmy was always fast asleep in the professionals' room. Yet whenever a boys' tournament was held, Jimmy would beat them all. In squash, he first challenged Donald Butcher for the Professional championship in 1933, but it took two more years to beat him. Dear would hold the Professional title for more than a decade (1935-47/50).

In 1935 he challenged the great Amr Bey for the British Open, the de-facto World championship. Dear lost, as he would again in their next two contests. Especially the second time was legendary, with former champion Butcher praising 'the astonishing, almost impudent, volleying of J. Dear, and the beautiful drops and lengths of Amr Bey. No match of squash rackets has ever compared for sheer beauty of stroke production'.

The phlegmatic Dear had great touch as well as smooth movement. After Amr retired in 1938, Dear won his only British Open title by beating fellow pro Albert Biddle. After the war Dear lost the next two British Open finals to Mahmoud Karim. By then squash was no longer Dear's primary focus, and he also won the World championship at rackets (1947-1954) and real tennis (1955-57); a unique triple record.

Dear playing Amr (right) in the British Open in 1935.

▶ The Premier Blue, Dear's autograph racket by Grays of Cambridge (c1935). By now most squash rackets that were produced were laminated like this one.

No vacancies

When Amr Bey retired in 1938 the British Open title became vacant. The association decided that Jim Dear would play one of the other professionals for the title. To determine who, an invitation tournament between five pros was held. In the final Albert Biddle (left), pro from the Junior Carlton Club beat Leslie Keeble (right), to become Dear's challenger.

Female pros

Most women who played squash in England in the 1930s were still from the upper classes and without a need to work. There were however at least two female squash professionals. The only one in London was Norma Williamson, at the St. Regis hotel; and in Liverpool Miss Lyon worked at the Adelphi. Both were teaching pros, not players of note. Until 1974 pros could not enter the Women's championship, the British Open ('Open' in this case meaning that women from outside Britain could participate).

▲ Silver gilded and enamelled pin, hallmarked 1938, for Grays, manufacturer of sports equipment. Jim Dear was an employee and friend of the Grays family, who believe this pin was a gift to him, in the year Dear won his British Open title.

GRAYS SQUASH RACQUETS ARE

"The Champion's Choice"

JIM DEAR
PROFESSIONAL CHAMPION OF THE BRITISH ISLES

GRAYS
of
CAMBRIDGE

SQUASH RACQUETS SPECIALISTS

DESIGNED & PRINTED BY NATHANIEL LLOYD & C° Lᵗᵈ LONDON

▶ Grays advertisement (1938) featuring Jim Dear.

The athletic Lumb dealing with a 'clinger' from Susan Noel in their 1939 final of the Women's championship.

Lady lightning

Margot Lumb was arguably the first female squash star. As a teen her father, a wealthy businessman had *'indefatigably'* coached her and her siblings in squash and other sports at their home court. In lawn tennis she became a British international, but she would excel even more at squash. Lumb (1912-1998) was a left hander with an attacking style, combining stroke play with exceptional pace. It was said that *'she moves about the court with speed, grace and purpose'*. In December 1934 she won her first Women's championship (better known as British Open).

Five only

Lumb would win the title five times in succession, winning each final 3-0. Runner up in the first two was the Hon. Anne Lytton-Milbanke, a tall strong player who relied on fitness and determination. In the next two Lumb met Sheila McKechnie (nee Keith Jones), who like herself had a graceful, fluent style. Then in her last final in 1939 Lumb beat former triple champion Susan Noel, who had come back from retirement, 9-6 9-1 9-7 in less than 30 minutes. As one reporter noted: *'Miss Lumb was remarkably fast in getting to shots that would have beaten anybody else'*. Only 26 years old, it's likely she would have won several more British Open championships if the war had not interfered.

Margot Lumb (top) playing at Queen's in 1934

Women get organised

The 1930s saw the forming of women's squash federations in the US (1930) and in the UK, where the Women's Squash Rackets Association (WSRA) was founded in 1934. That same year in the Australian state of New South Wales a regional women's association was formed. In Britain, new tournaments for women were also initiated, like the London Inter-Club competition, as well as many regional and county championships.

▼ Squash racket with telegraph pole press, both manufactured (c1930s) by the UK firm Murray & Baldwin.

Short vs skirt

At the start of the 1930s some British women began wearing shorts on the squash court, even during official matches. This caused quite a controversy at first, people being used to the knee-length (or longer) skirts of the 1920s. Within a few years shorter skirts as well as shorts became generally accepted, as Mrs Calvert Jones and Mrs Grant Taylor of the Prince's Club demonstrate in 1935.

▲ Cigarette card of Margot Lumb, handed out with packets of Hill's; from their 'Celebrities of sport' series (1939).

▲ Lumb receiving the championship trophy in 1939, with finalist Noel (far left) applauding.

The Streamline

The Hazells Streamline racket was invented by accident. The firm had been producing standard laminated rackets, but one day when workers returned from lunch, they noticed that on one racket the outer laminated strip had separated and sprung out. A patent for this shape (claimed to be more aerodynamic) was applied for in 1934. The lawn tennis version enjoyed some success thanks to Bunny Austin who used it at Wimbledon. A squash variant (a Red star model pictured) was also produced during the 1930s, but apparently only in very small numbers.

The squash racketeer

Cartoon from 'Keep your eye on the ball' (1936), an illustrated book of humorous poems on various sports. This one is about a squash ball being whacked around before taking its revenge on the racket.

Courts around the world

North America

Meanwhile Americans and Canadians continued to play their hardball variant. In the US, championships were started for professionals (1930, men), and for doubles (1933, men/women). But the main tournament remained the US Nationals, for amateur men, held since 1907. Pictured are the 1937 finalists, Germain Glidden (left, winner 1936/37/38) and Neil Sullivan (winner in 1934).

Germany and Sweden

Squash was already played in Germany by the British Army of the Rhine (BAOR), stationed there since 1919. In 1930 the first four German courts were built in Berlin for employees of the Siemens plant (pic). Several more courts appeared in Berlin in the 1930s, but the war ended all German squash until its rebirth in Hamburg in 1968.

In Sweden the first court was built in 1932 at a luxurious private home, Villa Åkerlund in Stockholm. A squash centre in Sveavägen opened in 1936, the year the first Swedish championship was held there. In 1937 new courts opened at Wittstocksgatan, today known as 'Stockholms Squash Klubb'.

Ireland and Wales

In 1932 Arthur Hamilton, a tennis and badminton international, won the first Irish squash championship. It was held at the Fitzwilliam Lawn Tennis Club in Dublin, where the country's first (club) squash court had been built in 1902. The first Welsh Amateur championship was won in March 1939 by Maurice Turnbull, a cricket and rugby international. Three weeks later Turnbull lost the challenge match for the Welsh Open championship against Haydn Davies, the country's only resident squash pro.

Sudan and Egypt

Throughout the Empire the British continued to build squash courts, like this open-air court (c1930s) at the Club in Wad Medani, Sudan, the centre of the country's cotton plantations, run by British officials.

In 1936 the first Egyptian championship (for amateurs) was won by Amr Bey at the Gezira Sporting Club, against a field of British players and two other upper-class Egyptians.

New Zealand and Australia

In New Zealand, Geoffrey Kingscote (pictured middle row, second right, with other contestants) in 1932 won the first men's National championship, having learned the game in England. The women would have to wait nearly 20 more years: Nancy New won the first NZ title in 1951. Australians were much earlier with Bettine Grey Smith, an all-round sportswoman and aviator, winning the first National women's championship in 1932.

CHAPTER 5

AFTER WORLD WAR II & DURING THE 1950s

Squash had already made inroads into the British Empire; and now alongside Egyptians, players from countries including Pakistan, India, Australia and South Africa were making the trip to the British Open and other British events after World War II. The 1950s would see the pre-eminence of the first generation of the extraordinary Khan dynasty, and the domination of the women's game by Janet Morgan.

AFTER WORLD WAR II & DURING THE 1950s

No boasts, just drives

During World War 2, Susan Noel, three times British Open champion and member of an aristocratic family, got up at 4am, cycled five miles to the depot and drove a bus from 5.30am until the afternoon each day – after filling the radiator!

Casualties of war

Three of the seven pre-war British Amateur winners perished during the conflict. Cyril Hamilton (1934 winner, pic) died in 1941 aged 31 while serving in the Army in North Africa; Victor Cazalet (1926/27/29/30) was a liaison officer killed in a plane crash in 1943 aged 46; while Kenneth Gandar-Dower (1938), an adventurer, was killed aged 35 by a Japanese torpedo on a boat near the Maldives.

The largest squash rackets club in the world . . .

Thames House, London

Thames House contains fifteen first-class squash courts, all of which were finished by Carters. The same firm has been responsible for almost **every first-class squash court in this country,** and about 90 per cent of the **standard courts.**
Carters will be pleased to send, at their own expense, a technical expert to advise you or submit estimates for Private, Club or Hotel Courts, or for the conversion of old buildings into courts. This free service they offer to anyone in the United Kingdom and most European Countries.
An illustrated brochure will be sent post free on request.

CARTERS SPORTS COURTS LTD.

Squash facilities were also war casualties

Thames House in London, with fifteen courts (shown in this 1936 advertisement) had been the largest club worldwide, but during the war the courts were seen as a good place to store files, and afterwards only three courts remained playable. Another of the city's main clubs, the Bath Club, was destroyed entirely by fire. The Queen's Club was bombed, though the squash courts miraculously survived.

First up from down under

Even before Geoff Hunt, Ken Hiscoe, Heather McKay and all those that followed, Gordon Watson (born in 1916) was the first Australian to make a mark internationally. In 1939 the Victorian became the first Australian Open champion. Not only was he to hold the title for the next ten years, including the war interruption, but he remained undefeated and only dropped a single game during the period. When British Open champion Mahmoud Karim travelled to Australia in 1949, Watson met him for the first time in the final of the Australian Professional championship. Watson reached 8-3 match ball in the deciding fifth game before Karim came back to take it 10-8 and with it the match.

Watson galvanised

Realising how competitive he could be, Watson was galvanised and he was funded to sail to the UK for the 1950 British Open, becoming the first Australian to do so. He managed to reach the semi-final which he lost to Abdul Bari from India, and was subsequently rated three worldwide behind Karim and Bari. Later, he not only coached many champions but managed centres, and as his Australian Hall of Fame entry says, Watson was '… *considered by many as a doyen of squash in Australia for 48 years, from 1931 to 1979',* when he retired from the game.

Gordon Watson pictured at the memorable final against Karim at the 1949 Australian Professional championship.

New Year revolution

New Year's Day 1954 saw the start of the first US Open. Although the draw was open to all nationalities, amateur or professional, the draw size was limited to 24 players. British Open champions Mahmoud Karim and Hashim Khan travelled to New York's University Club, for this hardball event, a format with which they were unfamiliar. Both progressed as they got used to the hardball game but Karim was beaten by US Amateur champion Henri Salaun (1926-2014, pic) in the semis. Khan got to the final by edging past another American Diehl Mateer in the semis before also going down to Salaun. Soon after Hashim Khan and other Pakistanis began to dominate the title as their adaption to hardball became more complete.

Portions of Curry, and Morgan's ten servings

The first thirteen women's British Opens after WW2 were shared by two Englishwomen. Played at the Lansdowne Club in London, Joan Curry took the first three and Janet Morgan the next ten. Morgan also lost in two finals to Curry, while Curry followed up her wins with three final losses to Morgan. This photo was taken of the two players (Curry, left) before the second of Curry's wins, in January 1948.

Best of British

Janet Morgan (1921- 2000) is arguably the best British female squash player ever – and a high-level tennis player too, competing at Wimbledon twelve times. How many British Open titles she could have won had she taken up squash before the age of twenty-five is an open question. Morgan had it all. She hit the ball harder than her opponents, she moved quicker and did not use a modified tennis swing. She used wrist 'snap' to add pace as needed, within her tactical armoury. She also had the distinction of being the first woman to add off-court training to her preparation, using her job as a physical education teacher to good effect.

Tennis and Squash magazine

In the summer of 1948 the British Lawn Tennis magazine, noting the increasing popularity of squash, reached agreement with the British Squash Rackets Association to make it their official publication and the title changed accordingly. It ran with squash until the start of Squash Player magazine in 1971.

Janet Morgan in action winning her second (of ten) British Open titles in 1951.

Morgan slams McKay

In 1955 Janet Morgan not only led the Wolfe-Noel Cup trans-Atlantic event winning British team, but personally achieved a grand slam of titles. She simultaneously held the British, US and Australian Open titles. Even Heather McKay didn't manage this record later as the titles were not all available to her to contest, despite McKay's record-breaking sixteen consecutive British Open crowns. Morgan was presented with this silver powder compact case by her 1955 British team members.

Steps to Sporting Fame · Joan Curry

Lawn tennis star and squash rackets champion is Patricia Joan Curry, born in 1920 at Sidmouth in Devonshire.

From knocking a ball about on the beach, Joan stepped up into serious lawn tennis when she was 16, and made such progress that she qualified for Wimbledon in 1939.

It was while engaged on war work that she took up squash in 1942, winning her very first tournament. She carried off the Women's Championship in 1947, 1948, and again in 1949.

One of the best of our women lawn tennis players, Miss Curry has made 1949 a memorable year by winning the English hard and covered courts singles titles against stern opposition.

▲ Newspaper comic from 1950 featuring Joan Curry.

WOMEN'S SQUASH RACKETS ASSOCIATION

THE WOMEN'S CHAMPIONSHIP

and

THE VETERAN'S CUP

to be held at

THE LANSDOWNE CLUB
Berkeley Square, London, W.1

from

Monday, 18th February

to

Saturday, 23rd February, 1957

PRICE . . . . SIXPENCE

'The' Championship

The Women's championship was played separately to the men's from its 1922 start until 1982; and until the 1970's didn't include the word British in its title. This is the programme for the 1957 championship, when Morgan won her eighth consecutive British Open title.

▶ Janet Morgan in 1953.

Joan Curry was the first post-war British Open champion before Morgan took over. Like Morgan, a tennis player too, but Curry had a game more built around retrieving. While she was genuinely an all-action player, before front wall photography began, action shots needed to be posed, not always realistically! Here Joan Curry vaults over American Elizabeth Pearson when Great Britain played USA in the Wolfe Noel Cup in 1950. Curry died, aged 101, in 2020.

Challenging times end

The last men's British Open played as challenge matches between just two players took place in December 1947. It was won by Egyptian Mahmoud Karim, who challenged the holder, England's Jim Dear and beat him two matches to nil.

Three months later Karim also became the first knock-out winner when the British Open was held again in March 1948, this time featuring a draw of sixteen players: nine professionals and seven amateurs. Karim and Dear both made it to the final, which Karim edged in a close match at London's Lansdowne Club 9-5 9-3 5-9 1-9 10-8; the second of Karim's four consecutive titles.

Elegance

Karim (1916–1999) the next in the Egyptian champion line after FD Amr Bey was a graceful mover and stylish stroke-maker who caressed the ball. He was generally summed up as 'elegant'. It was said he '... *hit it like a kid whipping a top, and it always died second bounce*'. His long reach, quick reactions and dominance of the tee made him so difficult to shift.

He had been introduced to squash while playing tennis and golf at the Gezira Club in Cairo, and he took to it so quickly and practised so hard that he soon became the squash pro there. As the court he played on had a concrete floor and no roof his success when introduced to a wooden floor was even more remarkable.

After being unbeatable for four years, his straight game losses to Hashim Khan in the 1951 & 52 British Opens spelt the end of his Open career. He moved to a coaching position in Montreal Canada, but such was his adaptability that he won the US Professional (hardball) title in 1957 & 58.

▲ Karim the great stylist in action in 1950.

91

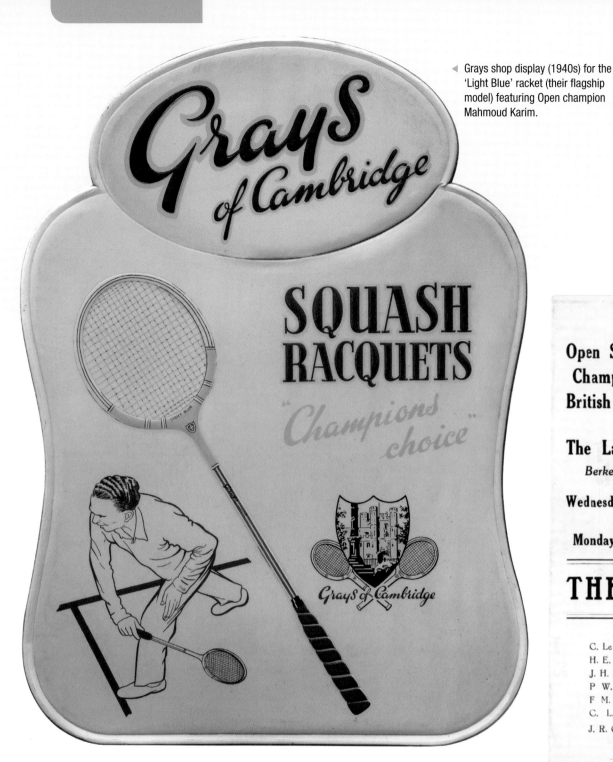

◀ Grays shop display (1940s) for the 'Light Blue' racket (their flagship model) featuring Open champion Mahmoud Karim.

Grays of Cambridge

SQUASH RACQUETS

"Champions choice"

Grays of Cambridge

Open Squash Rackets Championship of the British Isles, 1948-49

AT

The Lansdowne Club,
Berkeley Square, W.1

Wednesday, April 20th, 1949

TO

Monday, April 25th, 1949

THE DRAW

Stewards:

C. Le C. BROWNING
H. E. HAYMAN
J. H. HORRY
P W. Le GROS
F M. STRAWSON
C. L. STUBBS
J. R. C. YGLESIAS

▲ The draw for the 1949 British Open, when Karim won his third title. It was only the second year the championship was played as a knock-out tournament.

The first Administrator

September 1948 saw the British Federation, the Squash Rackets Association, employ a Secretary (manager) at their 25 Haymarket, London address. Henry Hayman, was the first full-time squash administrator for the SRA, then the de-facto world body.

Hashim begins
the Khan dynasty

Hashim Khan was the man who ended the British/Egyptian dominance of international events, and spearheaded the Pakistani success that followed. He started playing squash as a child at the Peshawar Club where his father Abdullah was chief steward. Afterwards Hashim took on a position as squash pro at the Pakistan Air Force base at Peshawar from where he dominated the Pakistani titles during the 1940's.

Then in April 1951 he arrived in London having been sent to try and win the British Open. Quite how old he was is uncertain – as he put it, *'Me not know how old I am, for reason me not born in hospital'*. But from the guessed date of 1 July 1914 that appeared on his passport it is definite that he was beyond his mid-thirties.

He was short, barrel-chested, balding, and with spindly legs, yet, at his first British Open final that month he demolished the tall and elegant champion Mahmoud Karim 9-5 9-0 9-0.

Holding the racket at the top of the grip, his speed was a sight to behold – it seemed there was nowhere on the court that an opponent could safely place the ball. Those whom he had dangling on a string may not have enjoyed the experience, but nobody could dislike the smiling and gracious champion.

1951 was the start of his reign as the undisputed top player, accumulating seven titles. Three times he went on to beat younger brother Azam in the finals, with only one blip, losing to cousin Roshan Khan (Jahangir Khan's father) in 1957.

Hashim showboats for the camera!

▲ HRH The Duke of Edinburgh, himself a keen squash player, presents the 1956 British Open trophy to Hashim Khan.

▲ After his playing career Hashim moved to the US, where he worked as a coach in Detroit, before he settled in Denver.

▲ Uniquely, all four men's semi-finalists in the British Open 1954 were related. They were L to R: Hashim, Abdul Bari, Nasrullah (who withdrew from the event), Roshan & Azam.

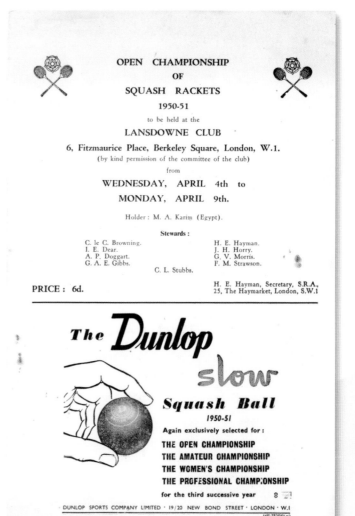

OPEN CHAMPIONSHIP
OF
SQUASH RACKETS
1950-51
to be held at the
LANSDOWNE CLUB
6, Fitzmaurice Place, Berkeley Square, London, W.1.
(by kind permission of the committee of the club)
from
WEDNESDAY, APRIL 4th to
MONDAY, APRIL 9th.

Holder : M. A. Karim (Egypt).

Stewards :

C. le C. Browning.   H. E. Hayman.
I. E. Dear.   J. H. Horry.
A. P. Doggart.   G. V. Morris.
G. A. E. Gibbs.   F. M. Strawson.
        C. L. Stubbs.

PRICE : 6d.   H. E. Hayman, Secretary, S.R.A.,
                   25, The Haymarket, London, S.W.1

The *Dunlop*
slow
Squash Ball
1950-51
Again exclusively selected for :
THE OPEN CHAMPIONSHIP
THE AMATEUR CHAMPIONSHIP
THE WOMEN'S CHAMPIONSHIP
THE PROFESSIONAL CHAMPIONSHIP
for the third successive year
DUNLOP SPORTS COMPANY LIMITED · 19/20 NEW BOND STREET · LONDON · W.1

▲ Programme of the 1951 British Open when Hashim won his first of seven titles.

◄ Dunlop squash ball box from late 1940s/early50s.

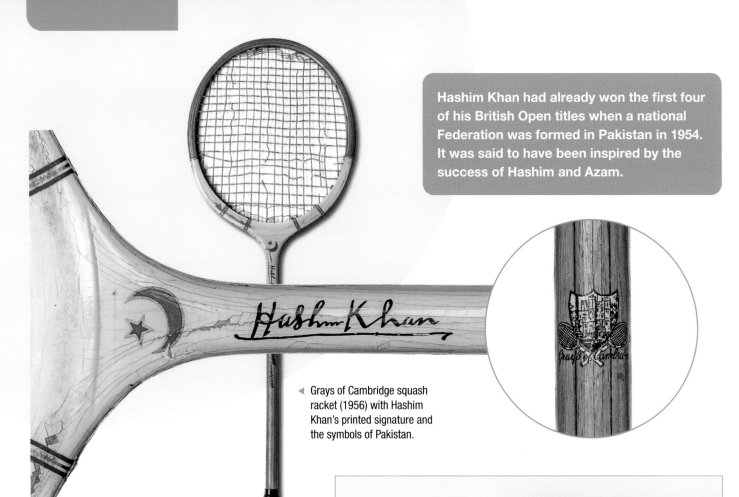

◀ Grays of Cambridge squash racket (1956) with Hashim Khan's printed signature and the symbols of Pakistan.

After Hashim came younger brother Azam who won four British Open titles between 1959 and 1961. More on him in the next chapter, but here he is shown (right) in a signed photo together with Hashim. ▼

In 1967 Hashim's book appeared, and was somewhat unusual and refreshing too, in that it featured his words, as he spoke them.

Examples include:

'Walls do not move, but ball … you need to watch, it moves.'

'When you see where opponent has idea to place ball, take big step in proper direction… Even you are high like Jolly Green Giant, take big step!'

'Cat never takes eye from bird it tries to catch and never you take eye away from ball you want to hit.'

'… I learn to breathe deep, always I try to suck in more air so I can stay running. I grow big chest, much room for air, and with rest of body small and light.'

'High-speed ball close to wall is hot potato, best you send it back quick.'

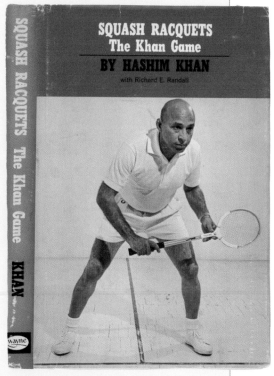

SQUASH RACQUETS
The Khan Game
BY HASHIM KHAN
with Richard E. Randall

SQUASH RACQUETS The Khan Game KHAN

Roshan Khan

Roshan Khan is famous for being the father of Jahangir Khan, but was in the vanguard of early Pakistani squash champions himself. He was assistant coach at the Rawalpindi Club when in 1951, aged 21, he won the Pakistan Professional championship, a title he was to retain for the next two editions.

Domestic politics conspired to prevent him travelling to England to compete, but when his new employers the Pakistan Navy funded him on the basis of winning the third Pro title, he was able to play the British Open. In the first two years Azam and then Hashim blocked his path in the semis, then in 1956 Hashim beat him in the final. But in 1957 Roshan prevailed, beating Hashim 6-9 9-5 9-2 9-1 to take the title.

Stroke maker

He may have only won one British Open title, but despite illnesses and leg injuries he took the Pakistan Professional title four times, won three US Open titles and two Canadian Open crowns. So Roshan fully deserves his place as a member of the great trio.

Roshan was the stroke maker who could retrieve too, while Hashim and Azam relied on their speed to a greater degree. It was only after he arrived in England that he underwent an operation to alleviate his deafness, and his charming personality emerged more easily.

After competing he returned to his pro position in Pakistan while also focussing on coaching sons Jahangir and Torsam.

▲ This photo was taken in 1955 when the three Khans, Hashim, Roshan and Azam (from L to R) went to the US together for the first time.

A relief for cats!

Although racket strings before the arrival of synthetic materials were called cat gut, the intestines of cats were never used. It was sheep and cows that were the providers. (It seems that the cat connection came from the stringed musical instrument 'kit', or the ancient Dutch name for real tennis 'kaats').

The first fifteen

Nations started forming national squash Federations in the first half of the 20th century. Here are the first fifteen Federated nations.

Federations formed:

USA*	1904
South Africa	1910
Canada*	1915
England	1928
Egypt	1931
New Zealand	1932
Australia	1934
Ireland	1935
Scotland	1936
Netherlands	1938
Wales	1938
Kenya	1952
Zimbabwe**	1952
India	1953
Pakistan	1954

*primarily hardball until 1970s

**earlier named Rhodesia

ROSHAN KHAN *British Open Champion*

The play of Roshan Khan, winner of the Open Championship of the British Isles (1957), showed a wonderful precision that reflected his choice of racket. He played with Dunlop Maxply, the racket built to add to its terrific power the precision that is the winning factor in championship squash. Balance, stringing, frame construction, selected materials : all have made Dunlop Maxply the world's most powerful and accurate squash racket.

* You've a choice of four squash rackets :

Fort Maxply . . . . **82/6** and **99/6**
(depending on shaft and stringing)
Blue Flash **70/-**
Matchpoint **60/-**
Alpha **49/6**
and two squash balls, slow or medium **35/5** per doz.

plays **Dunlop** *Squash Equipment*

IT'S THE FINEST!

▶ Dunlop advertisement from 1957 when Roshan Khan won his British Open title.

◀ Dunlop racket (c1957) featuring Roshan Khan. Over the years few racket models have been produced with a printed image of a squash champion.

THE KHAN DYNASTY

The most extraordinary family in World Squash

When Hashim Khan arrived in England in March 1951 to play in his first British Open it signalled a new era. An era of one Pakistani family dominating men's squash which lasted forty years, only seriously punctured by Geoff Hunt and Jonah Barrington. The extended family won 23 British Open titles between them. Great players, great coaches, great story!

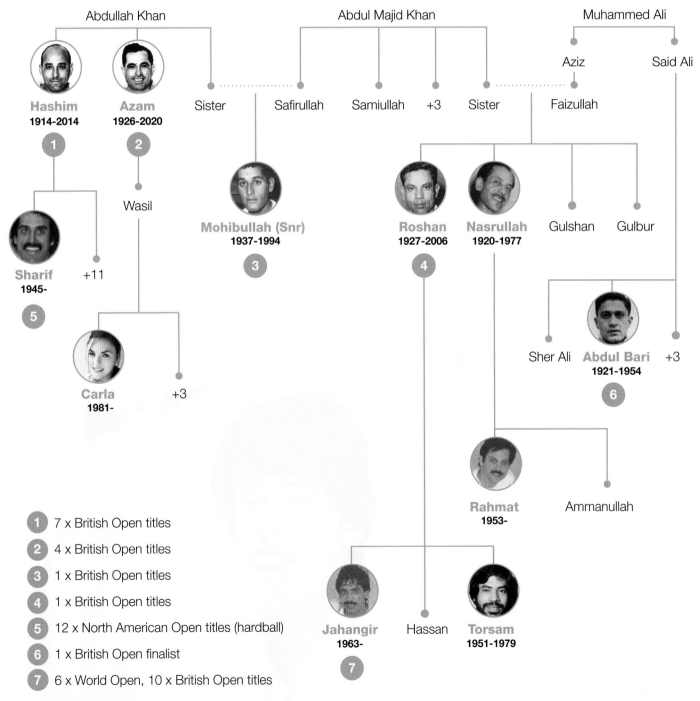

Abdullah Khan

Hashim
1914-2014
1

Azam
1926-2020
2

Sister

Wasil

Sharif
1945-
5

+11

Carla
1981-

+3

Abdul Majid Khan

Safirullah

Mohibullah (Snr)
1937-1994
3

Samiullah   +3   Sister   Faizullah

Roshan
1927-2006
4

Nasrullah
1920-1977

Muhammed Ali

Aziz   Said Ali

Gulshan   Gulbur

Sher Ali   Abdul Bari   +3
1921-1954
6

Rahmat
1953-

Ammanullah

Jahangir
1963-
7

Hassan

Torsam
1951-1979

1 7 x British Open titles

2 4 x British Open titles

3 1 x British Open titles

4 1 x British Open titles

5 12 x North American Open titles (hardball)

6 1 x British Open finalist

7 6 x World Open, 10 x British Open titles

Note: Early players did not always have birth certificates so dates are not definitive.
Dotted lines indicate marriage.

Squash stories from around the world

The Lansdowne Club

The Lansdowne Club in central London featured the named Bruce court, which at the time had a viewing capacity for 144 seated and about 60 standing. It was the home for most of the men's and all the women's major events from after the war until 1969. It was on this court that the Khans, Morgan and later Taleb and McKay won their British Open titles.

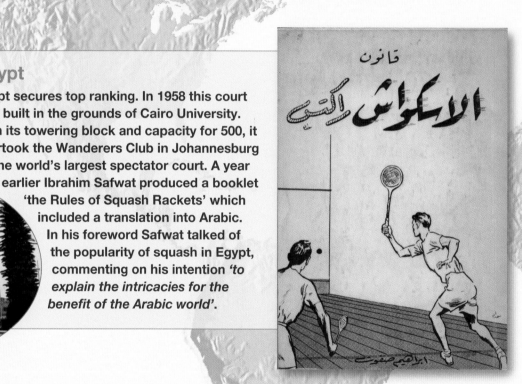

Egypt

Egypt secures top ranking. In 1958 this court was built in the grounds of Cairo University. With its towering block and capacity for 500, it overtook the Wanderers Club in Johannesburg as the world's largest spectator court. A year earlier Ibrahim Safwat produced a booklet 'the Rules of Squash Rackets' which included a translation into Arabic. In his foreword Safwat talked of the popularity of squash in Egypt, commenting on his intention *'to explain the intricacies for the benefit of the Arabic world'*.

Peak performance

Around 1950 in Kenya a few English expats built an open-air court, complete with backwall viewing platform on the slopes of Mt Kenya. The officials' 'station' where it was built was only five miles from the equator but at 6,000 ft high was cool. Especially slowed 'altitude balls' were a product of the future so their balls doubtless flew around the court back then!

Danish debut

A Men's team from Denmark landed in UK in 1949 to become the first national team from mainland Europe to do so. They played international matches against Scotland (0-5) and England (0-5). This first team (from L to R) were B.O. Smitt, H.E. Kastoft, C. Bauder, E. Bjerre-Petersen and O. Rasmussen.

Pay as you play

Australia in the 1950s was a pioneer in the building of public squash centers, on a 'pay as you play' principle (pic courts Frankston, Victoria). The international success of Australian top players in the next decades is often attributed to this.

South Africa

Gavin Hildick-Smith (foreground), was the first South African to achieve success on the international stage. A paediatric specialist, he won the British Amateur in January 1952 beating Englishman Brian Phillips (reaching upwards) in the final. He also reached the semi-finals of two British Opens, losing to eventual winner Hashim Khan each time.

Australia

In Australia in the 1950s squash continued to grow. Rackets like this 'Cressy' model (c1950) were being manufactured locally by the Alexander company. The first Australian squash books appeared by Mattick (1956) McCausland (1957) and by Napier (1957), who wrote the first full length instructional. Vin Napier was involved in many facets of Australian squash, not only as writer, player but also as coach (including 'discovering' Heather McKay), facilitator and administrator. Internationally, he would become one of the forces behind the formation of the World Federation.

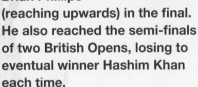

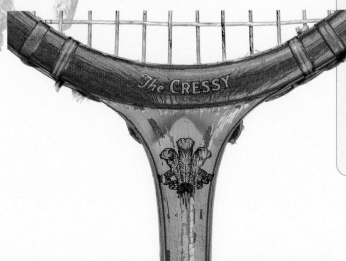

SQUASH IN THE 1960s

The domination of the Pakistani men and English women was ending with other nationalities coming to the fore, notably some Australian men and especially Heather McKay. The name Jonah Barrington was beginning to ring around the squash world. Squash administration at global level was being formalised and the first World titles were initiated. Squash was starting to become mainstream.

SQUASH IN THE 1960s
An incomparable record

The women's British Open began in 1922, but for the first 40 years no player from outside England had reached a final. Then, in 1962, Heather McKay (nee Blundell) arrived from Australia. Travelling to Scotland first she lost to England's Fran Marshall in the Scottish Open, but a month later overturned it to win her first British Open crown – and hold onto it for an unbroken sixteen years (1962 – 1977).

After her first win the British Lawn Tennis Magazine commented, *'How good is Miss Blundell? The answer is of course that she is not yet as good as she will be when experience is added to her already strong capabilities. Given time in which to perfect her drop shot and side wall play …'* Eighteen unbeaten years later it seems she did!

Heather McKay in 1968

Driving force
McKay (born 1941) was the eighth of eleven siblings, which meant that there was a lot of activity, but squash did not enter her life until she was 18 years old – to get fit for hockey! Contrary to expectations about a player who extraordinarily did not lose for so long, she was not physically imposing. Indeed, she was also shy and self-effacing off court. Instead it was the strength of her driving, her movement and relentlessness combined with so few errors that kept her ahead of the pack. As she explained, *'I was extremely lucky to be surrounded by positive and motivational people who were always willing to offer their support and encouragement and sound advice that I would then incorporate into my squash routine, with much success.'*

Heather McKay lost only two matches in her entire career (in 1960 and 1962) and maintained an unbeaten record from 1962 through to 1981 when she retired. This record included winning the first two World Open titles, held in 1976 and 1979, before returning in later years to win four World Masters titles between 1987 and 1993.

◄ Heather McKay holding the British Open trophy, a familiar sight for 16 years!

The un-named triple champion...

▲ This Spalding racket appeared in 1964 after Heather McKay won her third British Open. Some licence was used as there was no World championship until the next decade, the British Open being the unofficial world crown! As McKay was an amateur, she could not promote the brand with her name.

Between Morgan and McKay

Sandwiched between the Janet Morgan ten British Open wins in the 1950s and the unprecedented sixteen that Heather McKay began from 1962, two Englishwomen each grabbed the trophy once. In 1960 Sheila Macintosh (nee Speight) beat Fran Marshall in the final. Macintosh, who was a British international for over 20 years between 1949 and 1971 had lost five earlier finals to Janet Morgan.

▲ Fran Marshall (left) shown with Heather McKay, who is holding the World Open trophy in 1979.

And the following year Fran Marshall won her only British Open title, beating Ruth Turner in the final. Marshall would play four more British Open finals, losing each of those to the great McKay. But Marshall did enter the record books as being the last woman to ever beat her.

◄ Sheila Macintosh (left) with Janet Morgan in 1954.

The Dunlop Maxply

The Dunlop Maxply was one of the most iconic squash rackets of all time. A tennis version was first produced in 1930/31, and soon afterwards the first squash models followed. Named after their laminated, multiply construction, they were manufactured for well over 50 years, until in the 1980s wood was no longer used for squash rackets.

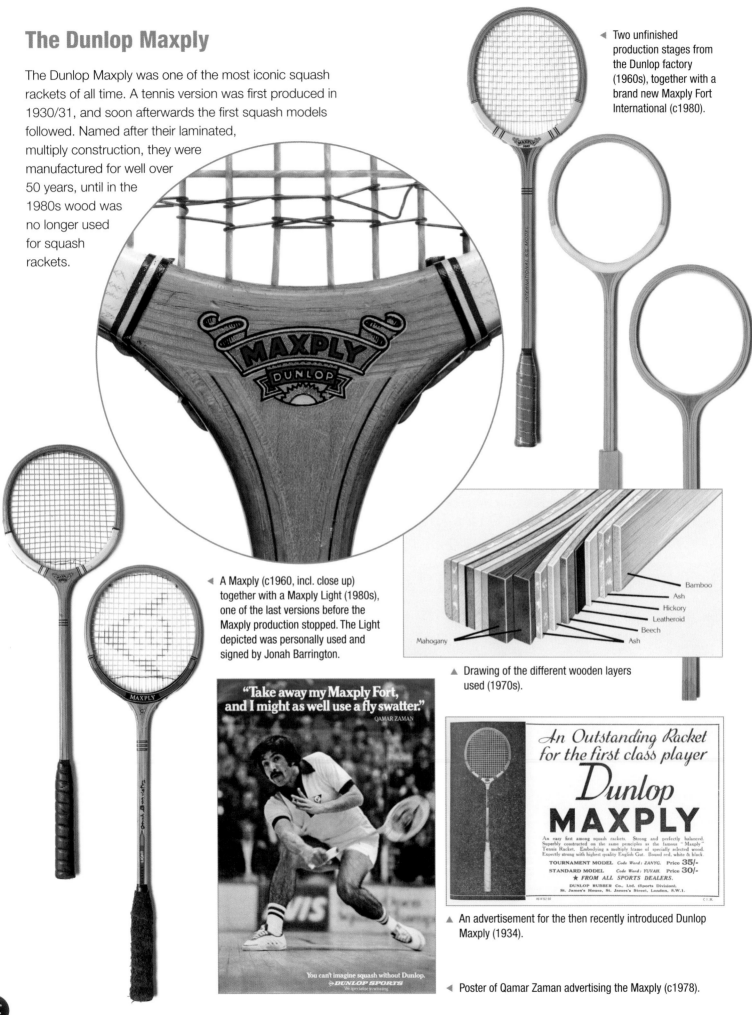

◀ Two unfinished production stages from the Dunlop factory (1960s), together with a brand new Maxply Fort International (c1980).

◀ A Maxply (c1960, incl. close up) together with a Maxply Light (1980s), one of the last versions before the Maxply production stopped. The Light depicted was personally used and signed by Jonah Barrington.

▲ Drawing of the different wooden layers used (1970s).

Bamboo
Ash
Hickory
Leatheroid
Beech
Ash
Mahogany

"Take away my Maxply Fort, and I might as well use a fly swatter."
QAMAR ZAMAN

You can't imagine squash without Dunlop.
DUNLOP SPORTS
We specialise in winning.

An Outstanding Racket for the first class player

Dunlop
MAXPLY

An easy first among squash rackets. Strong and perfectly balanced. Superbly constructed on the same principles as the famous "Maxply" Tennis Racket. Embodying a multiply frame of specially selected wood. Expertly strung with highest quality English Gut. Bound red, white & black.

TOURNAMENT MODEL   Code Word: ZANYG.   Price 35/-
STANDARD MODEL   Code Word: YUVAH.   Price 30/-
★ FROM ALL SPORTS DEALERS.
DUNLOP RUBBER Co. Ltd. (Sports Division),
St. James's House, St. James's Street, London, S.W.1.

▲ An advertisement for the then recently introduced Dunlop Maxply (1934).

◀ Poster of Qamar Zaman advertising the Maxply (c1978).

THE WOMEN WHO HAVE REACHED THE PINNACLE –
SQUASH'S WORLD TEAM CHAMPIONS

1979 GREAT BRITAIN
JAYNE ASHTON, ANGELA SMITH, SUE COGSWELL, LESLEY MOORE, BARBARA DIGGENS, TERESA LAWES

1981 AUSTRALIA
HEATHER MCKAY (MANAGER), RAE ANDERSON, VICKI HOFFMAN, BARBARA OLDFIELD, RHONDA THORNE

1983 AUSTRALIA
MARIE DONNELLY (MANAGER), CARIN CLONDA, JAN MILLER, DI DAVIS, RHONDA THORNE

1985 ENGLAND
LISA OPIE, LUCY SOUTTER, ALEX COWIE (MANAGER), MARTINE LE MOIGNAN, ALISON CUMINGS

1987 ENGLAND
LISA OPIE, MARTINE LE MOIGNAN, ALEX COWIE (MANAGER), LUCY SOUTTER, ALISON CUMINGS, SUZANNE HORNER

1989 ENGLAND
LISA OPIE, MARTINE LE MOIGNAN, ALEX COWIE (MANAGER), SUZANNE HORNER, ALISON CUMINGS

1990 ENGLAND
SUZANNE HORNER, LISA OPIE, MARTINE LE MOIGNAN, LUCY SOUTTER

1992 AUSTRALIA
LIZ IRVING, ROBYN LAMBOURNE, MICHELLE MARTIN, SARAH FITZ-GERALD, DI DAVIS (MANAGER)

1994 AUSTRALIA
CAROL OWENS, MICHELLE MARTIN, SARAH FITZ-GERALD, LIZ IRVING

1996 AUSTRALIA
LIZ IRVING, MICHELLE MARTIN, CAROL OWENS, SARAH FITZ-GERALD

1998 AUSTRALIA
DI DAVIS (MANAGER), LIZ IRVING, CAROL OWENS, SARAH FITZ-GERALD, MICHELLE MARTIN

2000 ENGLAND
STEPHANIE BRIND, TANIA BAILEY, LINDA CHARMAN, REBECCA MACREE

2002 AUSTRALIA
ROBYN COOPER, RACHAEL GRINHAM, SARAH FITZ-GERALD, NATALIE GRINHAM

2004 AUSTRALIA
NATALIE GRINHAM, RACHAEL GRINHAM, MICHELLE MARTIN (MANAGER), AMELIA PITTOCK, TESSA HINDS (PHYSIO), MELISSA MARTIN

2006 ENGLAND
ALISON WATERS, JENNY DUNCALF, TANIA BAILEY, VICKY BOTWRIGHT

2008 EGYPT
OMNEYA ABDEL KAWY, RANEEM EL WELILY, ENGY KHEIRALLAH, HEBA EL TORKY

2010 AUSTRALIA
SARAH FITZ-GERALD, KASEY BROWN, RACHAEL GRINHAM, DONNA URQUHART, MICHELLE MARTIN (MANAGER)

2012 EGYPT
OMNEYA ABDEL KAWY, RANEEM EL WELILY, NOUR EL SHERBINI, NOUR EL TAYEB

2014 ENGLAND
EMMA BEDDOES, SARAH-JANE PERRY, ALISON WATERS, LAURA MASSARO

2016 EGYPT
NOURAN GOHAR, RANEEM EL WELILY, OMNEYA ABDEL KAWY, AMR SHABANA (MANAGER), NOUR EL SHERBINI

2018 EGYPT
RANEEM EL WELILY, NOURAN GOHAR, NOUR EL SHERBINI, NOUR EL TAYEB

2022 EGYPT
NOUR EL TAYEB, HANIA EL HAMMAMY, NOUR EL SHERBINI, NOURAN GOHAR

www.squashlibrary.info

info@squashlibrary.info

Squash archive and information resource

Most photos kindly provided by Steve Line

Azam takes over from Hashim

Azam Khan's career came to an early full stop after winning his four British Open titles. His wins were recorded when it was played twice in 1959, then 1960 and 1961; but before he could go for a fifth he suffered a serious achilles injury. So it is a matter of speculation if he could have won more. Similarly, there is a debate as to whether he deferred to his older brother Hashim – Azam was runner-up to his brother three times before Hashim retired. It had been Hashim that had pushed him into giving up his tennis coaching job and to give squash a go; and from a standing start he improved so quickly that he was soon challenging Hashim. He admitted, *'I was hopeless at squash to begin with. I had no energy for the game, but Hashim kept telling me to stick at it and I would improve. Sure enough, I began to stay on court longer and longer without becoming so exhausted and my strokes improved too.'*

Watercolour painting of Azam Khan, made for an advertisement for Grays squash rackets.

Never hurried

Azam was summed up by Jack Giles, a contemporary, *'As a player Azam had everything. Small, compact and with a broad, deep chest he possessed great stamina. He moved beautifully, never appearing really hurried, yet covering all the court with deceptive ease.'* Such was his quality that after retiring from competitive play he would still easily beat current champions such as Jonah Barrington in practice at his base at the New Grampians Club in London where he was coach; and later the owner along with Hashim.

Although Azam was never as feted as Hashim, there was no resentment and the brothers were close throughout their long lives. In Azam's words, *'I have always been so proud of Hashim. He introduced me to squash, refused to let me quit through exhaustion in the early days and looked after me on my first trips abroad. I owe him everything, how can I possibly be jealous.'*

▶ Azam playing in the USA in 1955.

▲ Azam proudly holding the British Open trophy.

Shift in shafts

In 1956 the specifications of squash rackets changed. While the head still had to be made of wood, the shaft could be made from other materials. Here is a Dunlop Maxply made in Australia c1960, with a fibreglass shaft.

▲ New Grampians Club at Shepherds Bush, London where Azam was based.

Mike Oddy

Azam's New Grampians Club is where Mike Oddy from Scotland based himself. Khan's coaching gave him the tactical discipline needed to elevate his game, adding to Oddy's renowned single-mindedness and determination. The outstanding British player of his generation, Oddy beat holder Ibrahim Amin in the British Amateur final in 1961, and repeated the feat against the Egyptian the following year. All this managed by the Scot who had only one kidney.

Mike Oddy

Mohibullah Khan

Mohibullah Khan (Snr) was a postscript to the first Pakistani wave. In 1962 he beat emerging Abdelfattah Aboutaleb to win the British Open after losing three previous finals to Azam, his uncle. As with so many pros of the era, family relations had led Mohibullah into squash: he was a grandchild of Abdul Majid Khan, the rackets pro, son of Safirullah who taught him squash in Karachi, and nephew of Hashim and Azam who then took him under their wings.

His game featured more momentum than dedication, and after his British Open win 'Mo' settled in the USA at the Harvard Club in Boston – this was surprisingly facilitated by President John F. Kennedy whom he had met at an exhibition match. He enjoyed success in the hardball game, winning four North American Open and five US Professional titles, sadly passing away at the early age of 56.

Mohibullah Khan

Aftab Jawaid

Aftab Jawaid lost his first British Open final in 1965 to Aboutaleb, and would finish as runner-up on two more occasions. The tall, elegant and patient player had already become the first Pakistani winner of the British Amateur, taking the title three times (in 1964/65/66).

His success was thought to be an important factor in encouraging PIA (Pakistan International Airlines) to begin their long-term sponsorship association with squash.

◀ Jawaid's last event was the 1973 British Open where he beat debuting Qamar Zaman 3-2 before losing to Geoff Hunt in the quarter finals.

Abou emerges

In 1963 Abdelfattah Aboutaleb from Egypt won the first of his three British Open titles by beating Mike Oddy in the final. By doing so the Egyptian broke the thirteen year Pakistani stranglehold on the Men's British Open title begun by Hashim Khan. Only Ibrahim Amin, who had won the British Amateur twice (1956/60) and was runner up to Aboutaleb when his fellow Egyptian won his second title in 1964 had experienced some international success.

'Abou' as he was universally known, was possibly the greatest stroke maker who had graced a squash court up to that point; the crowd-pleaser regularly sprinkling unexpected and often outrageous shots. His career path was set by his brother, a Cairo tennis professional. His brother felt that he was too small to follow him into tennis and proposed squash instead. After serving his apprenticeship by sweeping courts and sneaking onto them, he grafted and eventually made it to the top of the national tree before travelling to compete. He may have been on the small side but had an inner strength as well as an external one, the latter burnished by pushing cars across sand in training! But strength alone does not equate to fitness as Abou found in 1966 when the triple British Open champion came up against Jonah Barrington, for whom fitness was everything. Abou subsided in the match as did his time at the top. Already stockily built he found it increasingly difficult to control his weight, although he did reach one more British Open final. His life was tragically cut short by a heart attack, at the age of 44.

Abdelfattah Aboutaleb

Scandi snatch

The British Junior Open Under 19 (named 'the Drysdale Cup') was considered the unofficial World Junior championship. From its start in 1926 it had only been won by British players, until Peter Gerlow from Denmark won in 1961 & 62, followed in short order by Sharif Khan (Pakistan) in 1963 and Anil Nayar (India) in 1965. (Left to right: Gerlow, Khan, Nayar).

Popping up from down under

Ken Hiscoe was the first man from Australia to win a major event. In January 1963 he went to the Lansdowne Club in London as fourth seed, and came away with the British Amateur title. This was six years before Geoff Hunt won his first British Open in 1969. Rugged, strong and resilient, Hiscoe had the full range of shots in his arsenal and used them all to repel the challenge from Egyptian Tewfik Shafik 9-3 9-7 5-9 9-7 in the final. But that was not the only Sydneysider's success. A trio of World Team titles came his way as a member of the Australian team that won the first three editions of the Men's World Team championship (1967/69/71); and he was manager/coach of the Australian teams that triumphed in 1989 and 1991. Oh, and the seven times Australian champion is credited with mentoring 16-year-old Geoff Hunt on his first trip to the UK, and in 1973 became the first President of ISPA, the men's players association.

Ken Hiscoe

Marriage then separation

When international team matches began in the 1920s, English players found themselves representing Great Britain for international test matches. A combined Great Britain team was also sent to the first World championships in 1967 and this continued until 1979. From 1981 England, Scotland and Wales entered World Team championships as separate nations.

SQUASH RACKETS
1969
GREAT BRITAIN

▶ Blazer badge of the Great Britain team of 1969.

Co-ordinating the world

International squash had been managed, as needed, by the British Squash Rackets Association (SRA), since its formation in 1928; but in the early 1960s calls for an international body began to be expressed. This impetus came at a time when there were already 36 National Federations administering squash in their own countries; and the idea was especially promoted by Australia and Egypt. Informal talks followed and, in January 1966, the SRA held a conference at its head offices in London to discuss planning a way forward.

The seven countries represented there were Australia, Great Britain, India, New Zealand, Pakistan, South Africa, United Arab Republic (Egypt); also present as observers were Canada and USA (both countries where the hardball squash variant was played). The agenda item read: *'Discuss the need to form an international federation'*, and according to the minutes the delegates were happy that the Federation be formed, and also proposed to start drafting an intended constitution. A year later, on 5 January 1967 the inaugural meeting of the International Squash Rackets Federation (ISRF) took place with representatives of the same seven nations. The constitution was accepted as drafted, and the seven countries were agreed as founder members.

▲ The same four Australian players won the first three editions of the World Team championship in 1967/69/71. They were left to right: Ken Hiscoe, Geoff Hunt, Dick Carter, Cam Nancarrow (here with Australian ISRF Representative Frank Boyle).

Men team up

Australia was appointed at the inaugural 1967 ISRF meeting to hold the first Men's World Amateur* championships (both a team and an individual event) later that year. [*Prior to the landmark ISRF decision that squash would go open from 1 Sept 1980, the sport was split between amateurs, essentially those that did not earn money directly from the sport, and those who did].

All the seven Founder member nations were lined up to compete in the inaugural team event in Sydney, but U.A.R. (Egypt) withdrew, so the remaining six nations played a round-robin in which Australia went unbeaten, beating favourites Great Britain on the way. Twenty-year old student Geoff Hunt proved to be a sensation, not only in the Australian team but also winning the individual event that followed. He would win this World Individual Amateur championship title three times in a row, from 1967 to 1971, before turning professional.

EARLY WORLD FEDERATION MEMBERS (Year of formation in brackets)	
1967	Australia (1934), Egypt (1931), England (1928), India (1953), New Zealand (1932), Pakistan (1954), South Africa (1910)
1969	Canada (1915)*, USA (1904)*
1971	Sweden (1965)
1975	Japan (1971), Kuwait (1968), Mexico (1968), Nigeria (1974)
1979	Finland (1971), Germany (West) (1973), Netherlands (1938)

▲ The New Zealand team at the 1967 inaugural World Team championship finished third behind winners Australia and Great Britain. Left to right: Charlie Waugh, Trevor Johnston, Peter Dibley, Don Burmeister.

* Offered founder member status retrospectively.

Jonah, a squash icon

When Jonah Barrington won the first of his six British Open titles in 1966 he did so as an amateur, and repeated this feat a year later. His becoming a professional was not just a turning point for him, but for the sport too. The Cornishman with an Irish father combined intensity, inspiration and charisma in such a potent blend that he almost single-handedly elevated the sport in the media, led to squash centres being opened, and the sport breaking out into the mainstream population. His application to training was unmatched, his determination to win all-consuming, his fluency laced with humour when talking to the media and the public, compelling. A man with a mission, he spearheaded the beginning of a professional player body and fought for prize funds to grow. The generations of professional players that have followed certainly owe much of their earnings to his evangelicalism.

▼ Jonah and his mentor Nasrullah Khan.

▲ An exhausted Barrington beat Geoff Hunt in the British Open final in December 1969.

JONAH BARRINGTON — will he become world champion?

A late starter

Surprisingly, Barrington (born 1941) had only started taking squash seriously at the age of 23. He had been dissolute at Trinity College in Dublin, but a lowly job at the SRA office gave him time to play ..... and to be taken under the wing of hard taskmaster Nasrullah Khan. This coaching brother of Roshan imposed a very strict regime, which Barrington embraced; ferociously training and giving up distractions. The light-weight left hander firmly believed that his training level would mean he would prevail against any player not putting in the same level of work or carrying any extra weight. His six British Open titles and his personality created a legend!

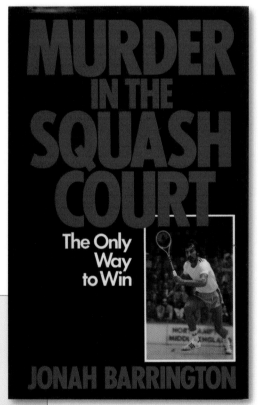

▲ The title says it all.... Barrington's seminal book.

Butyl Barrington

Another way in which Barrington changed squash was his successful campaign that pressured the authorities to move away from the very bouncy ball that encouraged attritional play. His efforts led to British manufacturers changing their specifications to the slower butyl Australian specification that offered more attacking options.

► Dunlop box from the late 1960s, with 12 butyl balls, individually wrapped. These 'slow' balls were used for tournament play.

THE MEN WHO HAVE REACHED THE PINNACLE –
SQUASH'S WORLD TEAM CHAMPIONS

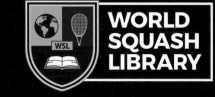
WORLD SQUASH LIBRARY

1967 AUSTRALIA
KEN HISCOE, GEOFF HUNT, OFFICIAL, DICK CARTER, CAM NANCARROW

1969 AUSTRALIA
KEN HISCOE, DICK CARTER, GEOFF HUNT, CAM NANCARROW

1971 AUSTRALIA
VIN NAPIER (MANAGER), KEN HISCOE, DICK CARTER, GEOFF HUNT, CAM NANCARROW

1973 AUSTRALIA
MIKE DONNELLY, DAVE WRIGHT, CAM NANCARROW, LIONEL ROBBERDS

1976 GREAT BRITAIN
STUART COURTNEY, JONNY LESLIE, IAN ROBINSON, PETER CHALK (MANAGER), PHILIP AYTON

1977 PAKISTAN
MOHAMED SALEEM, ATLAS KHAN, DAULAT KHAN, MAQSOOD AHMED

1979 GREAT BRITAIN
ANDREW DWYER, JONNY LESLIE, CHRIS STAHL (MANAGER), PETER VEROW, PHILIP KENYON

1981 PAKISTAN
QAMAR ZAMAN, MAQSOOD AHMED, GOGI ALAUDDIN, JAHANGIR KHAN

1983 PAKISTAN
MAQSOOD AHMED, QAMAR ZAMAN, JAHANGIR KHAN, GOGI ALAUDDIN

1985 PAKISTAN
SOHAIL QAISER, UMAR HAYAT KHAN, JANSHER KHAN, JAHANGIR KHAN

1987 PAKISTAN
QAMAR ZAMAN, JAHANGIR KHAN, KARAMATULLAH CHAUDRY (MANAGER), SPONSOR, UMAR HAYAT KHAN, JANSHER KHAN

1989 AUSTRALIA
RODNEY MARTIN, KEN HISCOE (MANAGER), CHRIS DITTMAR, BRETT MARTIN, CHRIS ROBERTSON

1991 AUSTRALIA
RODNEY EYLES, CHRIS ROBERTSON, CHRIS DITTMAR, KEN HISCOE (MANAGER), BRETT MARTIN

1993 PAKISTAN
JAHANGIR KHAN, JANSHER KHAN, ZARAK JAHAN KHAN, MIR ZAMAN GUL

1995 ENGLAND
SIMON PARKE, CHRIS WALKER, DEL HARRIS, MARK CHALONER

1997 ENGLAND
CHRIS WALKER, SIMON PARKE, PETER MARSHALL, DEL HARRIS

1999 EGYPT
AMR SHABANA, OMAR ELBOROLOSSY, AMIR WAGIH, AHMED BARADA

2001 AUSTRALIA
DAVID PALMER, RODNEY MARTIN, PAUL PRICE, JOHN WILLIAMS, STEWART BOSWELL

2003 AUSTRALIA
PAUL PRICE, ANTHONY RICKETTS, JOE KNEIPP, DAVID PALMER

2005 ENGLAND
JAMES WILLSTROP, NICK MATTHEW, LEE BEACHILL, PETER NICOL

2007 ENGLAND
LEE BEACHILL, NICK MATTHEW, JAMES WILLSTROP, PETER BARKER

2009 EGYPT
KARIM DARWISH, AMR SHABANA, RAMY ASHOUR, WAEL EL HINDI

2011 EGYPT
HISHAM ASHOUR, KARIM DARWISH, RAMY ASHOUR, MOHAMED ELSHORBAGY

2013 ENGLAND
NICK MATTHEW, DARYL SELBY, ADRIAN GRANT, JAMES WILLSTROP

2017 EGYPT
KARIM ABDEL GAWAD, RAMY ASHOUR, ALI FARAG, MARWAN ELSHORBAGY

2019 EGYPT
KARIM ABDEL GAWAD, TAREK MOMEN, ALI FARAG, MOHAMED ABOUELGHAR

2023 EGYPT
MAZEN HESHAM, ALI FARAG, YOUSSEF SOLIMAN, MOSTAFA ASAL

www.squashlibrary.info
info@squashlibrary.info

Squash archive and information resource
Many photos kindly provided by Steve Line
Prior to 1981 - World Amateur Team Championship

WORLD SQUASH LIBRARY

Testing times for women

In January 1963 the British team disembarked from the Queen Mary on their way to Philadelphia to take on the USA team in the 15th Wolfe Noel Cup. These trans-Atlantic test matches had begun in 1933, with the following one in 1968 being the last. (Left to right, back: Anna Craven-Smith, Pauline White, Fran Marshall, Mary Muncaster, front: Janet Morgan (non-playing captain), Sheila Macintosh, Claire Hargreaves, Jenny Crane).

The first women's test match between Great Britain and Australia took place in February 1964. The visitors included Heather McKay who had already won two of her sixteen British Opens, along with Jenny Irving, mother of future top player Liz Irving. The outcome at the Lansdowne Club in London was a 3 – 2 win to Australia.
(Left to right: Helen Plaisted, Heather McKay, Pat McClenaughan, Jenny Irving, Barbara Baxter).

▶ Before South Africa became excluded from international competition during the apartheid period, they hosted Great Britain in 1963. Then in 1968 the South African women travelled to the UK, including a tie at Edgbaston Priory in Birmingham where Sheila Macintosh (GB) is hitting an overhead against Gay Erskine (RSA).

▲ Original oil painting (1960) by Lawrence I. Toynbee. It demonstrates how by the 1960s squash was gradually becoming known by a wider public, including this renowned British artist, who usually painted popular sports like cricket and football.

Pane brings gain

The 1960s saw initial developments that would eventually transition squash into a real spectator sport.

The world's first squash court with a glass backwall was unveiled at Birkenhead Squash Rackets Club in Merseyside, UK in December 1966. It consisted of a panel of glass 5ft/152cm high by 16ft/488cm long let into the backwall; the glass being 1inch/2.5cm thick. However, as the wall opened onto a passageway viewing was negligible.

Next in 1968/69 entirely transparent backwalls were built in a new court at the University of Pennsylvania, USA; and the same was done in Brisbane, Australia. Unfortunately, the vertical steel mullions and head sections running the full width of the courts made spectating and filming difficult. So we move forward to 1971 in the next chapter for the first free-standing glass court backwall.

▶ A Slazenger shop display card (c1960).

Badminton or Squash

-better play with Slazenger

David Attenborough

At the time of the birth of glass back walls David Attenborough, the then BBC Director of Programmes and later world-famous natural historian, said this: 'So far we have not been able to convince ourselves that it is possible to follow this extremely fast-moving ball and still retain the essential geography of the game ..... we are very reluctant to embark on the coverage of a game without assuring ourselves that the coverage would be satisfactory.'

▲ A small glass window was placed in a court door at the Albert Park Squash Centre in Melbourne in 1965 to enable filming. It was used for the first Men's World Amateur championship in 1967, where Geoff Hunt (front) beat Cam Nancarrow (rear) in the final.

Hunt on the rise

As the decade came to an end, Australian Geoff Hunt had already begun to make his mark. In January 1969 he won the first of his eight British Open titles. His countryman Cam Nancarrow had beaten Jonah Barrington in the semi-finals so the Hunt / Barrington rivalry that had already begun, was not played out then. However, straight after the British Open they were pitted against each other in the World Amateur championships. First, Barrington beat him 9-7 in the deciding game in the team final, although Australia won 2-1 overall, before Hunt reversed that result in the individual event, winning 3-1.

◀ Geoff Hunt (right) and Jonah Barrington, the two great rivals, at the British Open in December 1969. On this occasion Hunt, the titleholder lost to Barrington in the final.

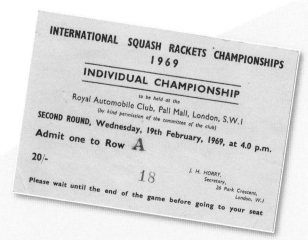

INTERNATIONAL SQUASH RACKETS CHAMPIONSHIPS
1969
INDIVIDUAL CHAMPIONSHIP
to be held at the
Royal Automobile Club, Pall Mall, London, S.W.I
(by kind permission of the committee of the club)
SECOND ROUND, Wednesday, 19th February, 1969, at 4.0 p.m.
Admit one to Row A
20/-
18
J. H. HORRY,
Secretary,
26 Park Crescent,
London, W.I
Please wait until the end of the game before going to your seat

CHAPTER 7

SQUASH IN THE 1970s

This decade saw great expansion, especially across Europe. In the UK Jonah Barrington led the media charge, and with it the building of facilities at pace – many now featuring the newly introduced glass back walls. World Open championships were beginning, and the professional men began managing their circuit. Australian legend Geoff Hunt was leading the way, but the next wave of Pakistani stars were nipping at his heels. Heather McKay was continuing her complete domination.

SQUASH IN THE 1970s
Men take charge

Up to this point the management of squash had been generally focused on the amateur game with professionals mainly coaching. They were unable to develop a pro tour themselves, which was an itch that Jonah Barrington set out to scratch after he turned pro. He tried to set up a touring troupe with limited success, but in February 1974, very unhappy with an event seeding imposed on them, players held a meeting in Birmingham, England.

That day the International Squash Players Association (ISPA) was formed, as Jonah Barrington explained after the meeting: *'Our simple aims are to co-ordinate as a professional players body and to protect that body's interests on an international basis; and to work with all the governing bodies, tournament organisations, and the sponsors to further safeguard the future development of competitive squash throughout the world.'* Barrington was appointed as ISPA Chairman, Ken Hiscoe as President, and Geoff Hunt as Vice President. Englishman Geoff Poole (pictured) was installed as first ISPA Secretary to oversee the administration. Once membership was initiated, ISPA began its own coordinated tour with events registering, being required to follow the Tour Rules that were evolved. ISPA evolved into PSA (Professional Squash Association) in January 1993 after it had merged with the World Professional Squash Association (WPSA), the North American hardball group, the previous year.

▼ Initially, ISPA produced periodic seeding lists before moving to ranking lists every two months in 1977. Monthly rankings debuted in 1998, before a move to weekly rankings in August 2022. This is an early seeding list dated September 1976.

1	Geoff Hunt	Australia
2	Mohibullah Khan	Pakistan
3	Gogi Alauddin	Pakistan
4	Qamar Zaman	Pakistan
5	Hiddy Jahan	Pakistan
6	Cam Nancarrow	Australia
7	Jonah Barrington	Ireland
8	Ken Hiscoe	Australia
9	Ahmed Safwat	Egypt
10	Torsam Khan	Pakistan
11	Mohamed Yasin	Pakistan
12	Billy Reedman	Australia
13	John Easter	England
14	Mohammad Asran	Egypt
15	Abbas Kaoud	Egypt
16	Ali Aziz	Egypt
17	Mohammed Khalifa	Egypt
18	Rahmat Khan	Pakistan
19	Bryan Patterson	England
20	Kevin Shawcross	Australia
21	Tony Hosford	Australia
22	Doug Stephenson	Australia
23	Shah Jahan Khan	Pakistan
24	Sajjad Muneer	Pakistan
25	Seiji Sakamoto	Japan

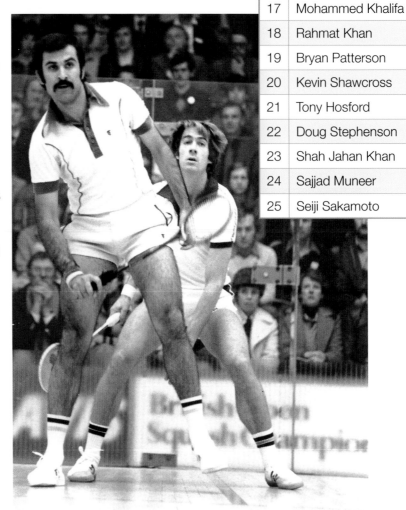

▶ Hiddy Jahan, 5th listed in 1976, was a top Pakistani player renowned as a hard hitter with a strong wrist. He reached the British Open final in 1982, when Jahangir Khan won the first of his ten titles, and later represented England.

THE MEN WHO HAVE REACHED THE PINNACLE –
SQUASH'S WORLD CHAMPIONS

1976.1977.1979.1980
GEOFF HUNT
Australia

1981.1982.1983.1984.1985.1988
JAHANGIR KHAN
Pakistan

1986
ROSS NORMAN
New Zealand

1987.1989.1990.1992.1993.1994.1995.1996
JANSHER KHAN
Pakistan

1991
RODNEY MARTIN
Australia

1997
RODNEY EYLES
Australia

1998
JONATHON POWER
Canada

1999
PETER NICOL
Scotland

2002.2006
DAVID PALMER
Australia

2003.2005.2007.2009
AMR SHABANA
Egypt

2004
THIERRY LINCOU
France

2008.2012.2014
RAMY ASHOUR
Egypt

2010.2011.2013
NICK MATTHEW
England

2015
GREGORY GAULTIER
France

2016
KARIM ABDEL GAWAD
Egypt

2017
MOHAMED ELSHORBAGY
Egypt

2019*.2021.2022.2023
ALI FARAG
Egypt

2019*
TAREK MOMEN
Egypt

2024
DIEGO ELIAS
Peru

www.squashlibrary.info
info@squashlibrary.info

Squash archive and
information resource

*Most photos kindly provided
by Steve Line*
*played twice in the year

Squash Info

WORLD
SQUASH
LIBRARY

THE SQUASH RESULTS
& ARCHIVE HUBS

In 1979 Heather McKay won her final World Open title.

Mighty McKay

The women's British Open allowed professional players to enter the tournament in 1974 having been restricted to amateurs before then. Winning her thirteenth title, Heather McKay was able to claim prize money for the first time!

American player Frank Satterthwaite summed McKay up in this way: *'Heather will simply never quit, and that, together with her technical ability, makes her not just the all-time best woman squash player but probably the most fantastic woman player in any racket sport — tennis, badminton, squash — who's ever lived.'*

▲ McKay in full control against Margaret Zachariah.

▼ Spalding Heather McKay racket from 1975, a year after she had turned pro

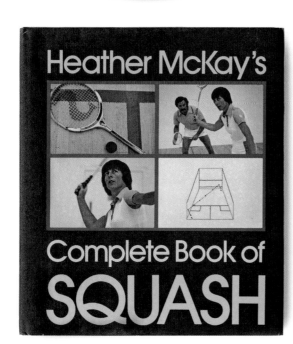

Sixteen and out

In 1977 Heather McKay won the last of her unequalled sixteen consecutive British Open titles. Played at the Wembley Squash Centre, she beat fellow-Australian Barbara Wall 9-3 9-1 9-2 in the final. Wall was the first unseeded woman to reach the final; it was also the first time both finalists were professionals. McKay had won all sixteen finals three games to nil and she only dropped two games during the whole period! The first two post-McKay editions would be won by fellow Aussies Sue Newman (1978) and Wall (1979).

Full set completed

Heather McKay took the opportunity to add *world champion* to her record when the first women's World Open took place in Brisbane, Australia in 1976. McKay and Geoff Hunt completed an Australian inaugural World title double, but hers was a much more straightforward win than Hunt's. McKay's final fodder was Marion Jackman, who was beaten 9-2 9-2 9-0 in 22 minutes; and indeed the 35-year-old only dropped sixteen points in the whole event.

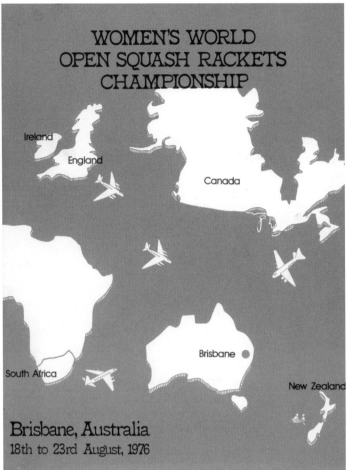

WOMEN'S WORLD OPEN SQUASH RACKETS CHAMPIONSHIP

Brisbane, Australia
18th to 23rd August, 1976

▲ In 1977, Heather McKay was ambushed for a TV programme called 'This Is Your Life' where the surprised person's life story is told via guests. Janet Morgan (Shardlow) who won ten British Open titles in the decade before McKay's domination was flown out to Australia to appear. Here they are together.

Women team up

It was another three years after the first World Open before the first Women's World Team championship was staged. The event was held in Birmingham, England, in 1979 for a trophy donated by the legends of women's squash, Heather McKay and Janet Morgan (Shardlow). McKay had come over from her retirement base in Canada to win the World Open title in Sheffield in the preceding days but did not continue breaking her retirement for the team event. Six countries entered the first edition, which was won by Great Britain on the only occasion before the Home Countries entered separately. The final saw GB beating Australia 3-0 with the remaining places going to 3rd Ireland, 4th Canada, 5th Sweden, 6th USA.

◀ Great Britain, the first Women's World Champions, clockwise from bottom left, Angela Smith, Jayne Ashton, Sue Cogswell, Lesley Moore, Barbara Diggens, Teresa Lawes.

THE WOMEN WHO HAVE REACHED THE PINNACLE –
SQUASH'S WORLD CHAMPIONS

WORLD SQUASH LIBRARY

1976.1979
HEATHER MCKAY
Australia

1981
RHONDA THORNE
Australia

1983
VICKI CARDWELL
Australia

1985.1987.1990.1992
SUSAN DEVOY
New Zealand

1989
MARTINE LE MOIGNAN
England

1993.1994.1995
MICHELLE MARTIN
Australia

1996.1997.1998.2001.2002
SARAH FITZ-GERALD
Australia

1999
CASSIE JACKMAN
England

2000.2003
CAROL OWENS
Australia / NZ

2004
VANESSA ATKINSON
Netherlands

2005.2006.2008.2009.2010.2011.2012.2014*
NICOL DAVID
Malaysia

2007
RACHAEL GRINHAM
Australia

2014*
LAURA MASSARO
England

2016, 2017*, 2019*, 2019*, 2021, 2022, 2023
NOUR EL SHERBINI
Egypt

2017*
RANEEM EL WELILY
Egypt

2024
NOURAN GOHAR
Egypt

www.squashlibrary.info
info@squashlibrary.info

Squash archive and information resource

Most photos kindly provided by Steve Line
played twice in the year

Squash Info

WORLD SQUASH LIBRARY

THE SQUASH RESULTS & ARCHIVE HUBS

Glass gets going

In 1971 Abbeydale Park Sports Club in Sheffield, England was the home of the first all-glass backwall installed using suspended assembly (i.e. with fins). It featured six panels and four fins. The British Open in 1972 was played on this new court, and it was used for the first BBC filming of the event in 1974. (Shown here when used in later years for the British Junior Open, right).

Broadcast news

Three years after glass backwalls using self-suspension first appeared at Abbeydale Park, the first court tailored for broadcast was constructed in 1974. It was the centrepiece of a 15 court pay-&-play facility at the Wembley Squash Centre in North West London (right).

For spectators, not only were there 240 seats behind the glass backwall, but also a gallery around the top of the court on the other three sides for an additional 100 spectators standing and watching over the walls just above the court lines. Seats in the middle of the tiered block could be removed for a TV camera. Additionally seats on both sides at the front were removable for cameras and a front wall 'camera pit' included for TV cameras along with photographers. Added to this was the provision of a commentary booth on the balcony.

Clear rears

There was a brief intermediate period at the end of the 1970s before four clear wall courts arrived during which temporary panel wall demountable courts with glass backwalls were used for events. The first was a Perstorp panel court at the Kungliga Tennishallen in Stockholm (pictured) in 1978 for a leg of the PIA World Series. It led to what was then reported as a world record major event audience of approaching 600 watching the final. The men's World Open in Toronto in 1979 used one too.

Shades of progress

White clothing (with trim accepted) on court was the general rule, before a short period when 'light pastel' shades were permitted. This only lasted until 1983 when the world body dropped colour restrictions entirely, leaving national federations/ clubs to set their own rules if they wished.

▲ Barrington floats a high serve.

Barrington bows out

Now into his thirties, Jonah Barrington won his last two of six British Open titles at Abbeydale Sports Club, Sheffield in 1972/73. Such was his appetite for competing that just months before his fortieth birthday Barrington took on holder Gawain Briars to win the 1980 British Nationals in the second year of it becoming 'open'.

Nobody pushed themselves harder. Barrington has been credited with inventing ghosting and used it extensively. It was even possible to tell who he was imagining playing as he went through various ghosting routines!

An elite director role with the SRA followed retirement and then squash coach at Millfield School. Mohamed Elshorbagy was sent there on a scholarship as a youngster, and emerged still being mentored by him as his stellar career developed. Barrington's intelligence, humour and intemperance, as much as his on-court achievements, have led Barrington to be arguably the strongest influencer the sport has seen.

◄ Even well into his thirties Barrrington was still a force to be reckoned with. Here he's taking on Zaman, more than a decade younger.

Dinner to honour
JONAH BARRINGTON
MBE

MONDAY 7th MARCH 1977 ● CAFE ROYAL LONDON W1

▲ Ascot Red Arrow racket from the early 1970s featuring Barrington.

◄ Amongst the widespread accolades that Barrington received for his sparkling career, a dinner was held in his honour by the National Sporting Club in London in 1977.

Hunt being filmed in action at Wembley.

▲ Smooth moving Hunt beating Zaman in the 1979 British Open final.

Hunt, endurance and enduring

Australian Geoff Hunt (born 1947) had a career that started in the 1960s, continued in the 1970s with him serially winning, and enduring into the early 1980s too.

His career can be summed up in these figures:

- Won 178 of 215 events he entered.
- Won 3 World Amateur Individual titles (1967/69/71).
- Won 4 World Open titles, including the first edition in 1976 (1976/77/79/80).
- Won 8 British Open titles (1969/74/76–81).
- Was Number 1 in the World listings for 59 months from their start in 1976 until 1980.
- Led Australia to 3 World Team titles including the first edition in 1967 (67/69/71).

Self-effacing both on and off court, it was clear to Hunt as he turned pro in 1971 that he should step up his training, placing his science degree and an intended research career on the back burner. And train, he certainly did. His ethos of going harder and longer, much like Jonah Barrington and later Jahangir Khan, set them apart from the pack. It was this strength of will, combined with his on-court movement that led to his outstanding career.

Hunt started to make waves even before his seventeenth birthday as a late addition to the 1963 Australian touring side. His potential was noticed then, and more so when he beat Ken Hiscoe to become Australian champion aged eighteen.

▲ Hunt on his way to beat Zaman in the British Open final at Wembley in 1978.

▶ Stellar Concorde racket (c1979). Hunt played with Stellar equipment and helped with their design, development and testing. Then after his playing career he was employed by the Australian company.

Perfectly oiled machine

Geoff Hunt was summed up by Jonah Barrington, saying *'There was nor never will be a better-balanced mover on court,…. as perfectly oiled a machine, so capable of producing the goods with such efficiency.'*

Perhaps the best example of the Hunt determination came when he won his last British Open in 1981, having lost to Jahangir Khan, then half his age of 34, at the Chichester Festival the week before. Hunt took the first two games but his tank seemed empty at 1-6 in the fourth game, the first three games having taken 106 minutes. Jahangir seemed spent too, and somehow Hunt found the strength to keep the rallies long and painful, induce mistakes and take his last title 9-2 9-7 5-9 9-7. Four games taking 134 minutes, but ending with him being helped off court and urinating blood!

The thoughtful demeanour of the man with a Bachelor Degree of Science gave an aura of shyness, but he could be forthright too, with views based upon analysis. So it was hardly surprising that it wasn't just his own on-court success that has led to a long post-playing career, not in science, but in coaching.

Two for one

The British Open played in 1976 at the Wembley Squash Centre in London saw the winner being awarded the first World Open title as a bonus! The final was the longest recorded match at that point, running for 130 minutes, and saw Hunt beating Pakistani Mohibullah Khan 7-9 9-4 8-10 9-2 9-2. Hunt went on to win the next three World Opens too.

Lucas
British Open Squash Championships
Incorporating the World Title

Wembley Squash Centre
31 January - 9 February 1976

▲ Barrington on the front foot against Hunt.

Federations everywhere

The European Union

The first continent to form a federation to represent the national federations within it was Europe. The European Squash Rackets Federation (ESRF) was founded on 27 April 1973 during the inaugural men's European Team Championship. These ten nations participated in that event in Edinburgh and became founder members: Denmark, England, Finland, Greece, Netherlands, Ireland, Monaco, Scotland, Sweden and Wales.

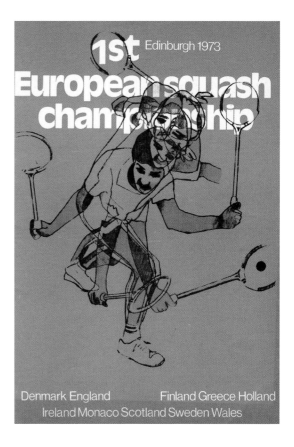

1st Edinburgh 1973
European squash championship

Denmark England   Finland Greece Holland
Ireland Monaco Scotland Sweden Wales

Mainland Europe Reported Courts 1974

Nation	Courts	Nation	Courts
Belgium	4	Monaco	2
Denmark	8	Netherlands	24
Finland	30	Norway	1
France	5	Portugal	1
Gibraltar	2	Spain	1
Greece	2	Sweden	185
Italy	1	Switzerland	5
Luxembourg	1	West Germany	7
Malta	6		

Regional Federation Founding Dates

1973: Europe • 1980: Asia • 1989: PanAm • 1992: Africa & Oceania

World Squash Federation Presidents

1967 - 1975	**Peter Phillips**	England
1975 - 1981	**Murray Day**	New Zealand
1981 - 1985	**Ian Stewart**	Canada
1985 - 1989	**Ronnie Sinclair**	Scotland
1989 - 1996	**H.R.H Tunku Imran**	Malaysia
1996 - 2002	**Susie Simcock**	New Zealand
2002 - 2008	**Jahangir Khan**	Pakistan
2008 - 2016	**N Ramachandran**	India
2016 - 2020	**Jacques Fontaine**	France
2020 -	**Zena Wooldridge**	England

Peter Phillips

Murray Day

Ian Stewart

Ronnie Sinclair

H.R.H Tunku Imran

Susie Simcock

Jahangir Khan

N. Ramachandran

Jacques Fontaine

Zena Wooldridge

Mr Squash

The 'Mr Squash' of his era, John Horry became the first full time CEO (then called Secretary) of the British SRA in 1955 when it was the unofficial world body. The Englishman then doubled up as the first Secretary of the fledgling world body itself (ISRF) when it began in 1967. He held the ISRF position until he retired in 1975, having stepped down from the SRA three years earlier, and received a national honour, an MBE, for Services To Squash (pic). Managing all the duties on his own, he did take on assistants who would do a little work while being given the opportunity to train. Jonah Barrington was one, Tony Swift and Mike Corby amongst others.

Pakistan's pursuing pack

The decade saw Jonah Barrington, and then Geoff Hunt especially, regularly needing to beat a band of elite Pakistani players standing in their path to titles. With the exception of 1977 when fellow Australian Cam Nancarrow was runner-up, Geoff Hunt beat Pakistani contenders in all of his seven other British Open final victories.

▲ Mo Yasin.

First was Mohamed Yasin in 1974, the busy player from Peshawar who had the ill-luck of having to withdraw before the final with an ankle injury having beaten Barrington in the quarter finals and Zaman in the semis. A year later in 1975 Hunt was beaten – by Qamar Zaman in the quarters, before Zaman lifted the trophy for the only time. Gogi Alauddin, the soft-touched tactician was that year's runner-up, as he had been to Barrington in 1973.

▲ Mohibullah and Zaman, long time sparring partners, friends and rivals.

▲ Mohibullah Khan Jr at the combined World/British Open championship in 1976, where he finished as runner up.

Then in 1976 for the combined British/World Open title the wiry and fit Mohibullah Khan was the runner-up (not related to Mohibullah Senior, this 'Mohi' was Jansher Khan's older brother).

Zaman lost to the Australian in three finals (1978-80), before 17 year old Jahangir Khan became Hunt's last victim. This defeat was Jahangir's last until the World Open in 1986. It was a similar story in the World Open. Hunt beat Mohibullah in the first in 1976 and Zaman in the next three finals.

▶ Zaman in the British Open final of 1978 which he lost to Geoff Hunt.

The PIA Squash Complex

The opening of the PIA Squash Complex in Karachi in 1976 enabled Pakistan to begin staging major events - and also to bring legends together, as this signed photo shows. Left to right: Azam Khan, Geoff Hunt, Hashim Khan, Jonah Barrington, Roshan Khan, Mohibullah Khan (Snr) and Qamar Zaman.

▲ Gogi Alauddin

Zaman... a wizard

Qamar Zaman, a nephew of 1970 British Open runner up Aftab Jawaid, is considered to be unfortunate not to have amassed more major titles. He may not have had the silky movement of others but his compelling racket-work led him to so many finals only to be blocked by Hunt. His squash career began in the Quetta Club in Pakistan where Hiddy Jahan's father was the squash pro and his own dad the tennis pro; and with PIA (Pakistan International Airlines) initially funding him as they recognized his potential. Before his 1975 British Open triumph his first trip to the UK saw him reach the British Amateur semi-finals in 1972.

Three times (1977/79/80) Hunt beat him in consecutive World Open finals, and a further three times in British Open finals (1978/79/80), even though Zaman had recorded several wins over the Australian. And when he surged again in 1984 for a final time to reach the World Open final aged 33 and before it the British Open final, Jahangir Khan thwarted him in both. His entertaining style, accompanied by an impish sense of fun, endeared him to audiences everywhere. An on-court interview conducted in English could spark a stream of Urdu to disconcert the interviewer; and referees would need to deal with humorous responses to their decisions or explanations. Zaman was quite simply a showman!

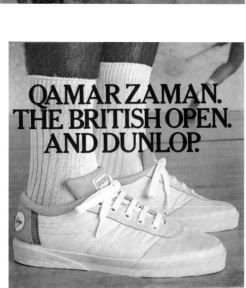

▶ Zaman at the British Open in 1975, when he won the title.

Sharif plays hardball

In the USA, Sharif Khan was the dominating player during the 1970s, picking up almost all titles. The eldest son of Hashim, he had been educated in England, initially enjoying success in (softball) squash, but it was in hardball that Sharif, with his fast and aggressive playing style, really excelled. He based himself in Canada, and would between 1969 and 1981 win no less than 12 North American Open and 9 US Professional championship titles.

Sharif Khan

▲ Hashim Khan delighting fans by playing Geoff Hunt in 1978, when Hashim won the British Open Over 65 event.

Now, a squash racquet made exclusively for women

The Lady Gray

Weighs only 7¼ ounces, with extra light balance and feel.

Natural gut gives the extra resilience.

Tough laminated wood shaft and frame, will stand up to the modern game.

Slim, well-shaped, light blue towel grip of about 3¼". Easier to grasp, more comfortable to hold.

A second model, the Gazelle, is available to the same frame specification, but with clear, synthetic stringing.

Grays of Cambridge
The Squash Specialists
Playfair Works Cambridge

▲ The first squash racket specifically produced for female players was the Lady Gray, launched in 1973 by Grays of Cambridge.

▲ In 1971, 18 years before the Berlin Wall stopped dividing Germany in 1989, two English internationals, Paul Millman (left) and Philip Ayton used it as a front wall on a promotional visit to Berlin.

The amateur game

British Amateurs

When the English Federation celebrated its 50th anniversary in 1978, a feature of the dinner held to mark the occasion was an assembly of top British players, nearly all winners of the British Amateur championship (pictured right).

World Amateurs

In the period between the formation of the ISRF and the sport going 'open' from 1980, each World Amateur Team championship was followed by a World Amateur Individual event. Geoff Hunt took the first three titles (1967/69/71) before he turned pro. Fellow Australian Cam Nancarrow followed Hunt as winner in 1973 having been runner-up to him twice, before another Australian, Kevin Shawcross (pictured right) triumphed in 1976.

In 1977 Maqsood Ahmed won; then in 1979 15 year old Jahangir Khan came through the qualification and took the World Amateur title. In 1981 the event would go 'open' and the individual title was discontinued altogether.

▲ Left to right: Philip Kenyon, Jonny Leslie (1980, the final edition), Philip Ayton, Jonah Barrington (67, & 68 twice), Mike Oddy (61/62), Nigel Broomfield (58/59), Roy Wilson (55/57), Alan Fairbairn (53/54), Norman Borrett (47/48/49/50/51), Dugald Macpherson (24/28).

Commercial centres spring up

While squash was already prevalent in the UK in public schools, universities, 'gentlemen's' clubs, sports clubs and forces bases, during the 1970s expansion leapt forward. The 'Jonah factor' promoted squash in the media and it became popular as a quick blast of exercise. In addition, local authorities provided courts looking for income options to offset costly public swimming pools. Not only were sports clubs adding courts but stand-alone commercial squash centres started springing up.

Racketball is born

Racketball is a more 'forgiving' form of squash, using a larger and more bouncy ball. It has been seen as an introduction to squash, a companion to it, and a game that can keep a little less supple players carrying on in later life too. Racquetball is similarly named and was being played on a court larger than a squash court with no tin in America before being adapted in the UK for squash courts in 1976. It started with pierced racquetball balls to slow them down. The British Racketball Association was formed in 1984, with some other countries adding it to their offerings too; with this branch of squash being formally renamed Squash57 in 2016 to set aside the racquetball/racketball confusion and fully identify it as a squash format.

Reading matters

The first squash magazine covering international news and results, came out of the UK in October 1971; and celebrated its 50th anniversary in 2021. The debut edition included coverage of the raising of the men's British Open winner prize money to GB£500, the shock surrounding Geoff Hunt turning pro, a profile of Jonah Barrington (cover photo), and the defeat of an attempt to end amateur status.

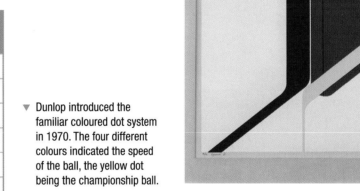

▶ Squash has even inspired abstract artists, like Knud Holar from Sweden, who made this serigraph (1973) titled 'Squash IV".

KEY WORLD CHAMPIONSHIP START DATES	
START	**WORLD CHAMPIONSHIP**
1967	Men's Team
1976	Men's & Women's Individual [1]
1976	Masters [2]
1979	Women's Team
1980	Men's Junior Individual & Team [3]
1981	Women's Junior Individual [3]
1985	Women's Junior Team [3]
1996	World Cup [4]
1997	Doubles [5]

1 World Open Championships
2 Stand-alone events from 1991
3 Under 19 age
4 Mixed team
5 Men's, women's, mixed

▼ Dunlop introduced the familiar coloured dot system in 1970. The four different colours indicated the speed of the ball, the yellow dot being the championship ball.

blue dot   FAST
red dot   MEDIUM
white dot   SLOW
yellow dot   EXTRA SUPER SLOW

CHAPTER 8

SQUASH IN THE 1980s

The 1980s was Jahangir Khan's decade of domination, but also the rise of countryman Jansher Khan in the later years. Meanwhile, Susan Devoy was pre-eminent in the women's game as the decade went on. It was a period of great change for the squash spectator with the arrival of showcourts, white balls and coloured floors. There was a revolution in squash rackets, with lighter materials and new shapes replacing traditional wooden rackets.

Jahangir celebrates
his British Open 1988 win.

SQUASH IN THE 1980s

Conqueror of the world

October 1979 saw a 15-year-old unknown Pakistani battle through the qualification and into the main draw of the World Amateur championship in Melbourne. He went on to win the event … and Jahangir Khan had arrived on the world stage. Having appeared, Jahangir, whose name means *conqueror of the world*, certainly did just that!

A few months later the now 16-year-old Jahangir gave Jonah Barrington a difficult time before losing in the third round of the British Open. At that time Jahangir (born 1963) was an introverted youngster who had endured the trauma of the death of his older brother Torsam on a squash court in Australia only weeks after his Melbourne triumph. Torsam had been his inspiration when he had regularly reappeared back in Karachi between competing in events around the world. Jahangir readily admitted that Torsam was his model, *'I played like my brother, and each time I saw him I copied him more'*.

Rahmat steps in

Jahangir acknowledged that the scintillating stroke play - which was the hallmark of his brother's game, was not the major facet of his own: *'I have style but not his craft,'* he explained. Born with a double hernia which made it seem unlikely that he would follow father Roshan and Torsam onto court, he defied expectations and did just that. Any style shortcomings were more than compensated by virtually incomparable power, stamina and inner strength.

The task of fulfilling Jahangir's potential was passed to cousin Rahmat Khan, a partnership that continued through his career.

▲ Rahmat advises.

▲ Torsam Khan on court with Ahmed Safwat.

Jahangir's career defined

His record-breaking ten consecutive British Open titles (1982-91) is a career benchmark.

Similarly extraordinary, his five-year, seven-month unbeaten run from April 1981 to November 1986, has been estimated to be over 550 matches. The end of this run came in the final of the World Open in Toulouse, France, when beaten by New Zealander Ross Norman.

ASK FOR THE CONQUEROR'S SHOES.

POWER
MAKES THE DIFFERENCE.

Jahangir Khan exclusively endorses Power Squash Shoes

▲ Seen here after his 1990 British Open win with his father Roshan who won the British Open in 1957.

◄ Wooden Unsquashable racket personally used by Jahangir during the 1983 British Open, which he won. The racket firm was founded by Rahmat Khan in 1977, and joined by Jahangir later.

Norman conquest

Ross Norman's World Open win over Jahangir at the Palais Des Sports in Toulouse 1986 was not only memorable in itself, but came with Norman's own backstory. It was not just that he had lost thirty consecutive times to Jahangir, but the victory came after he had been told by a specialist that he would be probably be unable to walk again. This diagnosis came after he landed awkwardly on the edge of the runway on his first parachute jump three years earlier. He severed one knee ligament, displaced another and reported *'it felt like falling out of a two-storey building'*.

Littered with comebacks

After the Norman defeat 1987 saw ten successive losses to Jansher, he was demoted to second position behind his namesake in the Pakistan team for the World championship in England. But Jahangir bounced back to win the World Open again in 1988, his sixth title; and he emerged in the following seasons to take three more British Open titles.

Finally, in November 1993, over two and a half years after his last British Open win, Jahangir Khan returned after injury and seeming retirement to reach the 1993 World Open final. He lost to Jansher, but the following day they joined up to spearhead Pakistan beating Australia in the final to win their sixth World Team title – on his home turf of Karachi. He then officially retired.

Once the playing chapter ended, another opened as he became a World Federation Vice President in 1998. After this, two terms as WSF President (2002-08) followed.

▲ Jahangir (left), on court with Jansher.

▶ Pakistan postage stamp, autographed by Jahangir.

▲ Jahangir dominates against Geoff Hunt.

Nearly three hours, only four games!

In 1983 top Egyptian Gamal Awad, nicknamed 'grasshopper' for the way he would flit around the court, was told by Jonah Barrington that he could beat Jahangir Khan by outlasting him. He tried, he failed. The first game of the Chichester Festival final took 71 minutes and the whole match (despite the marker muddling the hours on his sheet!) lasted 2hrs 46m. Jahangir carried on being unbeaten for nearly four more years, while Awad, a greatly talented and admired player, never quite recovered from the match.

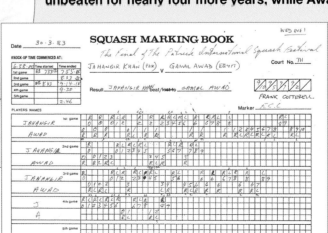

Wallpapering courts

Panelled glass-back courts that were demountable and so could be built and taken down within days, appeared in 1978 and were in use for events until the early 1980s, when courts with several glass walls started making an appearance.

For the World Open in 1981 at the Colombus Community Center in Toronto, Canada a court with two glass walls was used: a treated front glass wall in conjunction with a plain glass backwall and two demountable solid panel side walls, creating a 'tunnel' court. Also in 1981, a three-glass wall court was erected at the German Masters in Cologne.

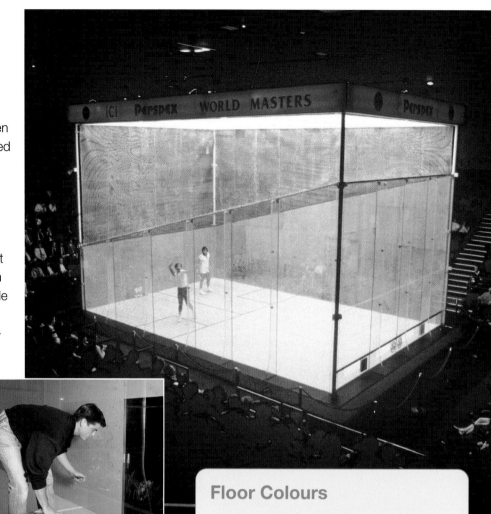

All-round viewing

Then in November 1982 a fully transparent court with viewing on all four sides made its debut. It was at the Granby Halls in Leicester, England (pictured) for the ICI World Masters (an event for professionals, not seniors). The walls of the Safe-Screen court were fabricated from Perspex.

All this new multi-sided viewing became possible with the invention of Contra Vision. Contra Vision, essentially a one-way view system, featured a clear sheet of superimposed black and white dots 'wallpapered' (pictured) onto the inside of the side and front court walls. The view into the court was clear but the players had a semi-opaque view outwards so that they could sight the white ball against the wall.

Floor Colours

The British Open led the way on floor colour changes following on from blue. Green was used as this was considered by broadcasters to be a 'warmer' colour for viewers, before a move to terra cotta inspired by clay court tennis. Coloured instead of black dots now enabled coloured walls to become an option too.

Pre 1984	**Natural wood**
1984 – 86	**Blue**
1987 – 92	**Green**
From 1993	**Terra Cotta**

Changing the score

Scoring points only when serving was the standard. However, in 1983 PAR (point-a-rally) scoring was trialled at a three-day event in Great Yarmouth, England, the Pro- Kennex Challenge. It used a best of 3 games to 11 points for the early rounds (and a three-point sudden death at ten all) designed for shorter, high incident matches. The men's tour moved to PAR in 1989 – initially to 15 points.

▶ The trialists (left to right): Philip Kenyon, Ross Thorne, Chris Dittmar, Hiddy Jahan, Gawain Briars, Dean Williams, Maqsood Ahmed.

Climbing a gantry

Referees were moved to be perched on a gantry erected against the backwall in 1984. The 'Squash Observer' was a perfect position for officiating, but not good when TV cameras were present as their back view obstructed the view of the court! While the gantry continued to be used in clubs, referees were moved back into the crowd at broadcast events.

A burst of colour

At the same time as colour was added to floors, the short period when the white clothing rule was relaxed to allow 'light pastel' was ended in 1983 when the world federation dropped colour restrictions entirely, making the sport more 'colourful' for spectators and broadcast viewers.

▶ Sohail Qaiser (left) and Rodney Martin embrace colour, as here in 1986.

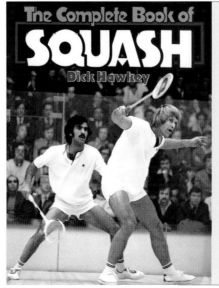

Dick Hawkey

Dick Hawkey has been the most prolific author of squash books, with fifteen titles to his name, ending in the 1980s. A British international (1954-59), he became a leading light in the technical, coaching and refereeing facets of the game, and these were his topics.

Vicki's victories, spurred by a loss

When the 1981 World Open came around, Vicki Cardwell (nee Hoffman, born 1955) had already won two British Open titles. Seeded one for the event in Canada, the 26-year-old was beaten by fellow Australian Rhonda Thorne in the final. Thorne won 8-10 9-4 9-5 7-9 9-7 in what was then a record-breaking 117 minutes, and the pinnacle of success for Queenslander Thorne.

The small, feisty left-hander from Adelaide then focussed obsessively on winning the next World Open two years later. First came success at the following two British Opens to complete the 1980-83 quartet of titles, before the 'major' re-match against Thorne in the 1983 World Open final in Perth, Australia. There, revenge was managed for the loss of eight points; after which she promptly announced her retirement to start a family.

Her determination to succeed was evidenced by her aggressive approach to training and playing. Along the way there were run-ins with authorities but she would not temper her forthrightness and enjoyment of a good celebration!

Second helping

A son and daughter already produced, aged 38 she re-joined the world tour and as she reached her fortieth year the former world number one reached a second ranking peak of twelve. Two years later she retired from the tour but her love of playing meant she continued to enjoy Masters success, winning world titles at 35, 45 and 55 age bands. Driven, demanding of herself, and addicted to simply playing, Cardwell was an Aussie great.

▼ Thorne (left) and Cardwell, rivals and World open winners

Susan Devoy in action, British Open 1986.

▲ Bryce Taylor advises.

New Zealand's golden girl

New Zealand's long squash history had produced a number of fine players, but it had to wait until 1985 for a small, slight player to give them their first women's world title. Susan Devoy (born 1964) had already engraved herself into 'majors' history, winning the 1984 and 85 British Open, beating Guernsey pair Lisa Opie and Martine Le Moignan, before arriving in Dublin in August 85 as top seed for the World Open. She did not disappoint, beating Opie 3-0 in the final, to win the first of her four World Open crowns.

Alongside these were eight British Open titles, five of which saw the Guernsey duo as runner-up, as they were in three of the four 'Worlds'.

However, it hadn't started well for Devoy. She had travelled to England aged 17, was based with later rival Opie in Nottingham, did not enjoy the cold and home-sickness she experienced, and the results were poor. *'I almost gave up then but my brothers would not hear of it',* she recalled. For the following season they arranged for her to go to Marlow, near London, to be under the wing of fellow Kiwi Bryce Taylor. With his coaching, and later management, she began to blossom.

Relentless

Relentless in training and on court too, packing power, pace and aggression; and with a long backhand drop that caused her opponents no end of discomfort. The only person that could beat her was herself, and Devoy did that occasionally. She became better at controlling her nerves and using them, but games were sometimes lost due to them, and a few matches too. And she could bristle when conversations took a turn she was not happy with, or shortcomings in details were noticed. Always direct was Devoy.

Finishing in Vancouver

A loss to Le Moignan in the 1989 World Open final and the quarters of the British Open to Sue Wright in 1991 were two blips in her domination, but Devoy stood atop the world rankings for eight and a half years; and was up there when the 1992 World Open in Canada came around. In Vancouver she dispatched Michelle Martin in the final, then twice more in the team event; tearfully announced her retirement in her victory speech. As with the rest of her career, her finish was on her own terms, leaving as one of the greatest women players in the history of the sport.

▶ Susan Devoy winning her fourth World Open title in 1992.

▲ Le Moignan in control in the 1985 British Open.

▶ Le Moignan (left) and Opie (right), looking relaxed.

Guernsey girls grab gold

Extraordinarily, two young women from the same 24 square mile island were major title winners. From the same school and squash club (there was only one on the island) they emerged from Guernsey to win British and World titles.

Tall, with an upright style and ripping boast, left-handed Martine Le Moignan upset Susan Devoy to win the 1989 World Open, and so become the first Briton to win a senior world title. Meanwhile smaller, deft and busier Lisa Opie had won the first World Junior individual title held in 1981, before beating Le Moignan in the semi-finals of the 1991 British Open, then taking the title with a win over holder Susan Devoy's conqueror Sue Wright in the final.

Together, they were members of the England squads which won the World Team title four times in a row (1985/87/89/90), sandwiched between Australian victories. While Le Moignan was serene, Opie was sometimes combustible caused by nerves and pressure, but both brought squash recognition to their small island.

Court snapshot 1987

The world federation produced this audit of squash clubs and courts in 1987 as a tool to show how worldwide the sport was, for the attempt to get squash into the Barcelona 1992 Olympics. It is perhaps noticeable that there were very few courts listed in South America; in Asia Korea is not shown; and Poland with two courts is very different from their current stock.

US goes soft

The US Open moved decisively from hardball to softball for the first time in 1985, when the Telegraph Hill Club in San Francisco hosted, with Jahangir Khan beating Ross Norman 15-4 15-5 15-8 to become the first softball holder.

IOC recognises squash

February 1986 was a milestone for squash as the IOC (International Olympic Committee) granted official recognition to the sport, thus admitting it into the Olympic movement. This was necessary so that bidding for a place on the Olympic programme could become possible.

INTERNATIONAL OLYMPIC COMMITTEE

INTERNATIONAL SQUASH RACKETS FEDERATION – MEMBER NATIONS

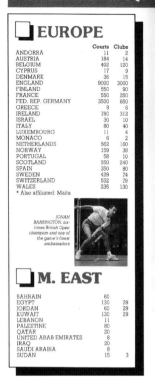

EUROPE	Courts	Clubs
ANDORRA	11	2
AUSTRIA	184	14
BELGIUM	402	120
CYPRUS	17	9
DENMARK	36	15
ENGLAND	9000	3000
FINLAND	550	90
FRANCE	550	250
FED. REP. GERMANY	3500	650
GREECE	9	6
IRELAND	780	312
ISRAEL	30	10
ITALY	80	40
LUXEMBOURG	11	4
MONACO	6	2
NETHERLANDS	562	160
NORWAY	159	38
PORTUGAL	58	10
SCOTLAND	650	240
SPAIN	350	80
SWEDEN	429	74
SWITZERLAND	552	79
WALES	235	130

* Also affiliated: Malta

JONAH BARRINGTON, six-times British Open champion and one of the game's finest ambassadors

M. EAST	Courts	Clubs
BAHRAIN	60	
EGYPT	130	29
JORDAN	60	29
KUWAIT	130	29
LEBANON	11	
PALESTINE	80	
QATAR	20	
UNITED ARAB EMIRATES	8	
IRAQ	20	
SAUDI ARABIA	8	
SUDAN	15	3

ASIA	Courts	Clubs
BANGLADESH		
BRUNEI		
HONG KONG	260	29
INDIA	150	
INDONESIA	50	20
JAPAN	60	
MALAYSIA	650	119
MUSCAT & OMAN	45	26
PAKISTAN	212	3
PHILLIPINES	25	
SINGAPORE	500	71
SRI LANKA	8	
THAILAND		

AFRICA	Courts	Clubs
KENYA	80	
NIGERIA	350	
SOUTHERN AFRICA	1900	429
ZAMBIA	31	
ZIMBABWE	116	42

CARIBBEAN	Courts	Clubs
BAHAMAS	15	2
BARBADOS	14	2
BERMUDA	10	4
TRINIDAD & TOBAGO		
GUYANA		
JAMAICA	15	5
ST. VINCENT & THE GRENADINES	8	1
CAYMAN ISLANDS	2	1
ST LUCIA		
ANTIGUA		
DOMINICAN REPUBLIC		

N. AMERICA	Courts	Clubs
CANADA	1800	375
MEXICO	150	
U.S.A.	3500	243

S. AMERICA	Courts	Clubs
ARGENTINA	500	100
BRAZIL	65	
COLOMBIA		
CHILE		
ECUADOR		
PARAGUAY	12	6
PERU		
URUGUAY		
VENEZUELA	5	

TWO of the most talented players on the world circuit, Australia's Rodney Martin (left) and New Zealand's Stuart Davenport

OCEANIA	Courts	Clubs
AUSTRALIA	6000	900
NEW ZEALAND	691	256
PAPUA NEW GUINEA	38	10

Amateur status abolished

A landmark decision taken by ISRF (now WSF) at its meeting in Brisbane, Australia in October 1979 was that the sport of squash would become open. Until that point the sport was split between amateurs, essentially those who did not earn money directly from the sport, and professionals who did.

The motion was worded: *'That ISRF adopt the principle of Open Squash … and be authorised to implement the necessary changes to enable the above principle of Open Squash to take effect from 1st September 1980'.*

So the World Team championships which followed the decision were open, and the World Amateur championship ceased to be held.

The British Amateur championship had begun in the 1922/23 season attracting the best players from around the globe; and finished when the sport went open, with the last one ending on 4 February 1980. It was won by England's Jonny Leslie who beat Ross Norman (NZL) in the final. He is pictured here with 1924/28 winner Dugald Macpherson.

Grey is gone

The greyness of showcourts was first eliminated in March 1983 when a coloured (blue) floor appeared at the French Open at the Cirque d'Hiver in Paris. A white ball debuted there too as another milestone on the road to making squash presentation more attractive to broadcasters.

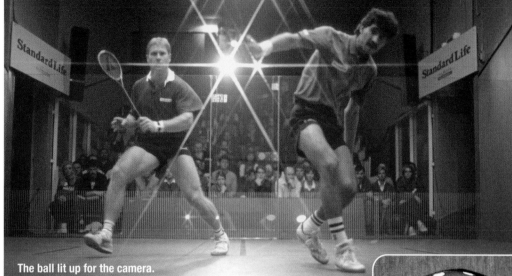

The ball lit up for the camera.

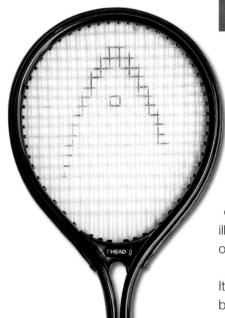

Dentists drill

White balls and coloured floors were improving ball visibility for broadcast, but the idea of two dentists from Carshalton in Surrey, England was tried too. They drilled Dunlop balls to make indentations, much like the dimples in golf balls, which they filled with retro-reflective material (pictured top right). Lights mounted next to the TV cameras would shine on to the ball, with light bounced straight back into the lens, illuminating and so 'enlarging' the ball. It used the same principle of cats-eyes in roads lit by car headlights.

It was tried at the 1985 British Open, and did produce glowing balls, but hampered viewing through the front wall as spectators were looking directly into the strong lights. A variation of the theme using fingers of material rather than dots was used on Merco balls for the 1986 World Open in Toulouse, France (pictured bottom right). However, the increased proportion of reflective area to rubber made it more prone to skidding. The photos show the difference made when the ball is 'lit'. It was soon phased out as the lights were so intrusive.

New materials

The Head Professional was the first approved squash racket made of one-piece tubular aluminium. Before this, all squash racket heads still had to be made of wood. Head developed this aluminium racket, together with a graphite racket (the Competition) in close cooperation with the squash associations, and with their official approval they were introduced in 1982. The relaxing of the rules by the ISRF allowed other firms to also use these new lighter materials, and this spelled the end for wooden squash rackets.

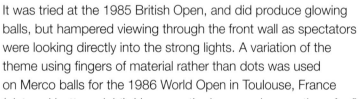

The second JK

Even as Jahangir Khan was in his pomp, the next Pakistani 'legend' was on his way. One from Jahangir's own country, indeed his own village of Nawakille. It was Jansher Khan.

Jansher's father was a store-man at a Pakistan Airforce base so his squash inspiration came from his brothers: Mohibullah, who had reached world number two; and Atlas, who was also a high flyer and member of the Pakistan team that won the world title in 1977.

His own squash life started by watching Mohibullah and Qamar Zaman after school, and occasionally getting on court with them too. The youngest of eleven siblings, he was not encouraged to play. *'When I started playing squash, my parents and everyone else did not want me to play because they considered me to be too feeble to endure the constant demands of this fast-paced game. This did not deter me but instead made me more resolute to play competitively'* he said.

Becoming a phenomenon

Jansher (born 1969) won the Pakistan national Under 19 title aged 13, and the Asian Junior when 16; and indeed took a game off Jahangir at the Pakistan Open that year. But it was when he started to beat Jahangir Khan in 1987 that he became a phenomenon. Jansher won the first two (of his record total of eight) World Open titles in 1987 & 89, and his career blossomed into the 1990s.

▲ Jansher (left) and Jahangir Khan compete.

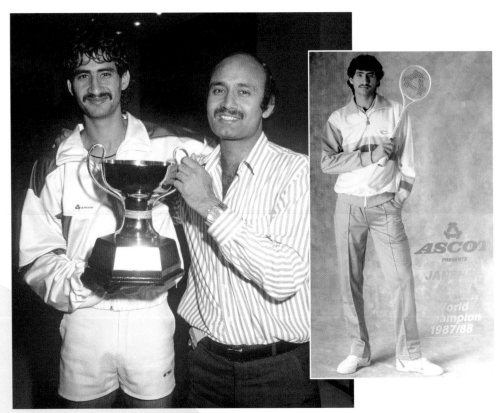

▲ When Jansher won the 1989 World Open, brother Mohibullah was on hand to share the moment.

Royal Albert Hall

Audience numbers rose and peaked at the Royal Albert Hall in London for the Men's World Team championship in 1987 where 3,526 watched a session, and Pakistan, led by Jansher and Jahangir, took the team title.

The best player never to...

Many sports have them - the best player not to have won their pinnacle titles; squash's arguably being Australian Chris Dittmar. His problem was being a contemporary of Jahangir and Jansher Khan. After Jahangir beat him in the 1983 World Open final, Jansher did so four times (1987/89/90/92). He would normally need to beat both to take major titles, a feat he came tantalising close to achieving in Malaysia in 1989 when he beat Jahangir 15-13 in the fifth game in the World Open semis; and going two games ahead against Jansher in the final before subsiding.

The left-hander from Adelaide who prowled the court like a graceful big cat also lost in two British Open finals. However, there was consolation in being a member of the Australian team that won the World Team title in 1989 and 1991; and a number of major international titles as well as taking the top world ranking in July and August 1993.

◀ Jansher vs Dittmar.

▼ Jahangir Khan defeated Chris Dittmar in the 1985 British Open final when Dittmar was aged 21, before Jansher Khan beat him in the Australian's second final eight years later in 1993.

157

Various rackets from the 1980s

The 1980s was a decade of experimentation for squash racket manufacturers. This was not only due to the rule change allowing new materials (other than just wood), but was also caused by innovations in tennis rackets. It resulted in a variety of squash models, sometimes with strange designs.

Wooden rackets, due to the adding of other materials, could take on different shapes (left to right): Goudie Eros (open throat), Grays Light Blue Executive (teardrop shape), Pro Kennex Q (lopsided), Grays Royal (flattop, diagonally strung).

▶ Dunlop balls and tin from the c1980s.

New materials, designs and production processes were also applied (left to right): Montana (alu/titanium), Dunlop Max500GS (injection molded graphite), Shark (off set squared head, privately produced in association with squash pro Danny Lee, graphite), Sp.in S-2 (longer strings but legal because these did not enlarge the playing area, graphite), Völkl S1 (two-coloured stringing, V shaped throat, epoxy/graphite/fiberglass).

159

Women form a federation

During the first women's World Open championship in Brisbane, Australia in 1976 a meeting between players and administrators agreed that a separate players organisation for women was needed at international level; and while an attempt was made to begin an independent body in 1978 it did not take hold.

Back in Australia, a player gathering at the 1983 World Open decided that the women should follow the men and institute WISPA (Women's International Squash Players Association). The following year on 26 February 1984 its first general meeting was held. New Zealander Robyn Blackwood (left) was elected as first Chair, with Australian Rae Anderson (right) becoming Secretary/Treasurer.

The male and female player bodies merged under the PSA name on 1 January 2015.

Togetherness

In 1982, on the 60th anniversary of the first women's event, the men's and women's British Opens were staged together for the first time. It saw the first of ten triumphs of Jahangir Khan, and the third of four wins for Vicki Cardwell.

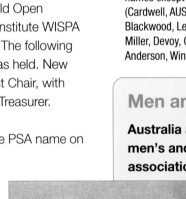

END OF BRITISH SEASON - APRIL 1983

DIVIDED BY 5 (or number of tournaments played if more than 5.)

1.	Vicki C.	92.8
2.	Lisa O.	80.0
3.	Robyn B.	53.4
4.	Martine L.M.	52.1
5.	Thonda T.	48.5
6.	Sue C.	44.6
7.	Angela S.	41.2
8.	Barbara D.	32.0
9.	Jan M.	27.8
10.	Susan Devoy	26.6
11.	Carin C.	25.4
12.	Renee A.	25.3
13.	Rae A.	23.0
14.	Lynne F.	21.8
15.	Alex C.	19.2
16.	Paula A.	16.0
17.	Gill W.	11.8
18.	Jayne A.	10.6
19.	Nicola S.	5.8
20.	Claire O.	3.0
21.	Lucy S.	0.6
22.	Lesley M.	0.6

Communication is encouraged.

The proposal for women professional players to join I.S.P.A. was sent to Mr. Peter Lucke-Hille on 25.4.1983. A reply was received by Rae Anderson on 19.5.1983 stating that :

"he will be meeting the Board of Directors shortly (!? my addition) to discuss how we should approach the whole thing".

Also enclosed is the letter sent to S.R.A.'s all over the world so that you know what is happening.

Regards,

RAE J. ANDERSON,
On behalf of interim committee.

▲ The first women's ranking list, shown here, missing family names except Devoy, and nations too! Topping it was Vicki C (Cardwell, AUS). The family names in order: Cardwell, Opie, Blackwood, Le Moignan, Thorne, Cogswell, Smith, Diggens, Miller, Devoy, Clonda, Aucamp, Anderson, Ferry, Cowie, Anderson, Winkler, Ashton, Spurgeon, Oxley, Soutter, Moore.

Men and women combine

Australia and England had separate men's and women's national associations until both amalgamated during the decade. The Australians joined up in 1981 after the women had been separate for 29 years. The English women amalgamated with their male counterparts in 1989, 55 years after their start in 1934. However, both were preceded by the USA women, who joined their male counterparts in 1979.

▲ SRA President Norman Borrett and WSRA President Ann Jackson cement the English deal.

World titles for juniors

The decade began with the first men's World Junior team and individual titles being contested in 1980. Australian Peter Nance was the first individual winner, while his team took that title. Indeed Australia won five of the first seven editions taking place in even years.

The Women's Junior began in 1981, but only as an individual event initially. That year, Lisa Opie prevailed over Martine Le Moignan in an all-Guernsey final. Australia won the inaugural women's World Junior Team event in 1985 – which was held alongside the Women's event. The junior team (J) is seen here with their senior counterparts who finished third. (Left to right) Back: Jan Miller, Tracey Smith, Di Davis, Danielle Drady (J), Michelle Martin (J), Sarah Fitz-Gerald (J). Front: Sally Ann Robbie (J), Carin Clonda, Margaret Zachariah (J manager).

Until 2009 each World Junior Individual only took place every two years alongside the respective team events. From then on the individual events became annual; and in 2025 the team events will move to an annual basis too.

New Zealand

Dardir El Bakary made his mark as one of the most influential coaches from the 1960s onwards. This was not just in his native Egypt but also included spells in Australia, England and especially New Zealand. As well as coaching many top stars there he has also been credited with kickstarting the development of so much of the New Zealand elite structure. He worked with rising stars Bruce Brownlee, Ross Norman and Susan Devoy. Brownlee was the first New Zealander to win a major title, when he took the British Amateur crown in 1976. Turning pro, he reached the world's top six, but was forced into early retirement in 1981 aged 26 with a severe hip problem.

The Extender – Dominant Power and Delicate Touch combined in a unique design

The Extender is a revolutionary new racquet from Prince. The unique teardrop head shape increases the length of the vertical strings, giving a power zone more than 20% larger than conventional racquets.

At 6¾ ozs, the Extender is ultra light too, increasing head speed and manoeuvrability.

The result – a measured 12% more power in a racquet which is lighter and more powerful than anything you've ever tried before.

You'll feel the difference in your quicker reflex shots, the ability to execute tough gets in the corner and the overall feeling of controlled power.

Not strong enough? Don't believe it. Like all Prince squash racquets, the Extender is guaranteed for six months

against breakage in normal play.

The Extender will help you improve your game whether you're a beginner or an international – ask your Prince stockist for details of our unique 4 Game Trial Offer.

Prince racquets revolutionised tennis – now we're shaping the future of squash.

prince®
LET THE GAMES BEGIN.

▲ In 1988 Prince launched their revolutionary Prince Extender, with its extended long strings and its teardrop shape. It opened up the market for oversize rackets, and other manufacturers soon followed.

▲ Dardir seen here with Jonah Barrington in 1988.

▶ Brownlee moves forward against Hiddy Jahan.

CHAPTER 9

SQUASH IN THE 1990s

While the Khans, especially Jansher, were still dominating the men's game for most of the 1990s, players from other continents began to make their mark, including Jonathon Power as first North-American. Women's squash was headed by Australians Michelle Martin and Sarah Fitz-Gerald. Squash's worldwide footprint was increasing and the sport started to be included in major games. Iconic show court venues, not least a court in front of the Pyramids, emerged.

▲ Michelle Martin played Suzanne Horner (nee Burgess, rear) in the 1993 British Open final.

SQUASH IN THE 1990s

Martin family affair

The Australian Martins, Brett, Rodney and Michelle, made squash a highly successful family business. Their sports pedigree not only came from their father, a state tennis player, but mother Dawn as well. She won national masters tennis titles; and her brother Lionel Robberds was a national squash team member – and an especially important mentor to Michelle.

Michelle makes it to one

It was Michelle (born 1967) who had the biggest trophy cabinet of the family. Three World Open titles (1993/94/95) and six consecutive British Open wins (1993-98) were highlights, as was winning Commonwealth Games gold when squash made its debut in 1998 (along with a second gold for Mixed Doubles), and 56 other tour titles from 85 final appearances.

One of the greatest female players of all time, she held the world number one spot for a total of 58 months between March 1993 and her retirement at the end of 1999. She also led her country to success in four successive World Team championships (1992/4/6/8).

▲ Brothers Brett and Rodney celebrate Michelle's first British Open win.

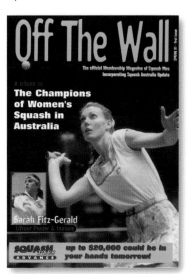

Uncle Lionel

A sparkling career, but the female Martin who, like her brothers, appeared dismissive to strangers, did not find it easy to reach the top of the rankings pole. As she said, *'I knew I had the potential to reach the top spot, but I lacked the physical and technical aptitude'*. So, it was 'uncle Lionel' she turned to; and under his guidance she was transformed into a consistently high performer.

Her attacking game would overwhelm opponents but Robberds (above) ensured discipline too. She needed to improve her racket preparation and footwork to effectively deal with higher calibre opposition; and working with Robberds she developed these over time. Later, when Rodney retired, he took over the coaching role to his sister and they became a close partnership as she tweaked her game to stay on top until her retirement aged 32.

▲ Martin's moment of triumph over Fitz-Gerald at the 1998 Commonwealth Games.

▲ Michelle's service action on the cover of an Australian squash magazine in Spring 1997.

Rodney's memorable home win

Older brother Rodney (born 1965) had already reached three British Open finals (1988/89/90), losing all to Jahangir Khan, before he reached a personal pinnacle at the World Open in Adelaide in 1991. There he became the only player to ever beat both Khans in the same event. To take the title he defeated Jansher in the quarters, Jahangir in the final, with Chris Dittmar sandwiched between them in the semis.

He may not have seemed 'giving,' not being very outgoing, but that masked a wry sense of humour. Rodney was tricky and inventive. His slim frame, upright stance, short grip and cocked wrist made him instantly recognisable. His strengths beyond gifted stroke-making: almost clinical accuracy and a steely determination to win, would have carried him to more success but for a hip injury that caused his early retirement.

▲ Rodney Martin lining up his shot.

◄ Rodney Martin's volleying puts Jahangir Khan under pressure.

Different animal

Brett, the oldest sibling (born 1963), was a different animal altogether. He may have lifted the men's World Team trophy in 1989 and 91, but while Rodney was interested in constructing rallies, it was shorter the better for Brett. Unorthodox and deceptive on court, taciturn to the point of shyness off it, he was able to hold a place in the world top ten for a decade, and in 1994 reached the number two spot, as Rodney had done – both blocked from number one by Jahangir and Jansher Khan.

▶ Brett Martin's wrist action keeps Chis Walker guessing.

The evolution of the squash racket

Top to bottom, in date order: Prosser & Sons racket (c1910, solid wood), Head Competition (1982, apparently the first officially approved graphite), Prince Extender (1988), Head Genesis 440 (1991), Tecnifibre Carboflex 125NS Airshaft (2021).

Early squash rackets were shaped after rackets rackets. A single piece of wood (usually ash) was steam bent and joined at the throat with a wooden wedge in-between. These solid wooden rackets remained the standard for squash until the late 1920s. Then laminated squash rackets rapidly came into vogue. This was possible after the invention of new resin glues for the aircraft industry. Several layers of thin strips of wood were glued together, creating a much stronger racket.

Squash rackets still had to be made of wood, but in 1956 other materials were first allowed, although for the shaft only. It was not until the early 1980s that racket frames entirely made of new, lighter, materials as aluminium or graphite (carbon fibre) were permitted. The shape of the squash racket head was at that time still more or less the same as it had been a century earlier. That changed in 1988 with the arrival of the Prince Extender, with its teardrop shape. The next step was the Head 440 racket in 1991, when these much larger strung surfaces (up to 500cm2) first became allowed. The lighter materials combined with larger racket heads have had a great impact on the way squash has been played since then.

The glass court close to the Giza Pyramids in Cairo, first used in 1996.

Egypt's new wave

After a period in the doldrums, the start of the revival of Egyptian international squash success can be traced back to Christchurch in New Zealand in 1994. There, Ahmed Barada beat Omar Elborolossy to win the World Junior title, before they teamed up to guide Egypt to the Junior Team trophy for the first time.

At the end of the decade, in 1999, squat Barada and rangy Elborolossy would link up with Amir Wagih and 20-year-old rising star Amr Shabana to win the first men's World Team championship for Egypt. Soon Egyptian players would start to dominate the men's world tour, to be followed by the women.

▲ Ahmed Barada, the first Egyptian to reach a World Open final, in 1999 when he lost to Peter Nicol.

Programmes to develop women's squash in Egypt began in the 1990s led by Dr Samiha Abou Magd. By 1993 the trio of Salma Shabana (Amr's sister), Maha Zein and May Hegazy entered the World Junior Team championship, and finished in 3rd place. The following year saw the same three and Heba Abou Ouf become the first Egyptian Women's Team championship entry. They finished 14th but the effort made to develop girls' squash bore fruit with junior success leading to players winning senior titles too.

▶ Dr Samiha (left) and coach Ahmed Safwat with the 1st women's team in 1994 (left to right): Hegazy, Shabana, Abou Ouf, Zein.

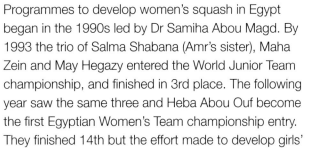

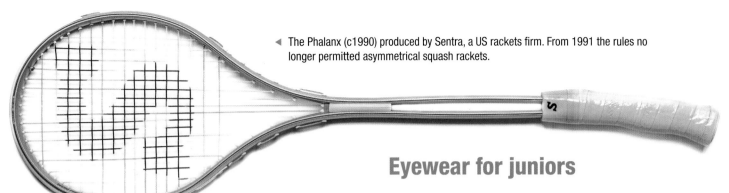

◄ The Phalanx (c1990) produced by Sentra, a US rackets firm. From 1991 the rules no longer permitted asymmetrical squash rackets.

Eyewear for juniors

Players in close proximity, swinging rackets and hitting small balls, brings with it a small chance of a ball or racket frame in the eye. In 1999, the WSF made wearing certified protective eyewear mandatory for doubles events and junior events, leading to nations insisting that all youngsters must use eyewear whenever on court.

▲ Juniors Nicol David (left) and Vicky Lankester in 1999.

Leaving a mark

A feature of white court walls has always been dark marks left by balls, especially from skiddy boasts near the back wall. 'Non-marking' balls tried to address this but only to reduce, not eliminate, the problem. The protective strips at the top of rackets also marked the walls, leading to the WSF squash racket specifications being amended. Since 1994, these *'bumper strips' have to 'be white, colourless or unpigmented'*, with colour only permitted if they were non-marking.

Dots doubled, larger sizes too

Soon after the second World War manufacturers started to offer a range of squash balls with different bounce/speed levels, from slow to fast. From 1970 onwards this difference was indicated by coloured dots: from the yellow dot, the slowest ball used for competition, to the fastest ball, the blue dot. Then in 1999 market leader Dunlop launched the double yellow dot as their slowest. At the same time they introduced slightly larger balls for beginners and improvers as indicated on the ad.

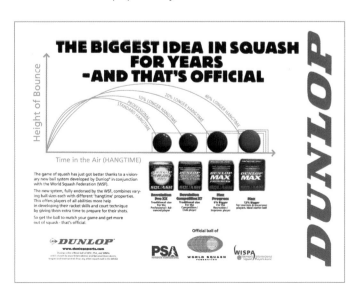

Jansher blossoms while Jahangir concludes

A series of wins against Jahangir in 1987, including a memorable four game victory in the World Open semi-final, cemented Jansher's position atop the rankings. Self-confident and sometimes too relaxed, he let a few matches slip, but was always focused for the majors. His record breaking eight World Open titles (1987/89/90/92-96) and six British Open wins (1992-97) shows that.

He also spent a record 97 months in the world number one spot, won 99 tour titles and was a member of the Pakistan World Team championship winning team in 1985/87/93. Winning his third team gold, he was supported by Jahangir Khan in what was Jahangir's swansong.

A wiry frame, consummate court coverage built around blinding speed, and an armoury of winners that were added to his basic running game made him almost unstoppable. What had been termed feebleness before, was now a lightness that made it seem that he floated over the court floor. Almost languid but with a durability that would wear any opponent down was his oeuvre. There is no doubting his status as a great of the game.

Meanwhile, Jahangir Khan won his tenth and last British Open in 1991, and while he made a comeback from injury to reach the World Open final in Karachi in 1993, he lost the all-Pakistani match to Jansher Khan 14-15 15-9 15-5 15-5.

▲ Jansher in control against Zarak Jahan Khan at the British Open 1996.

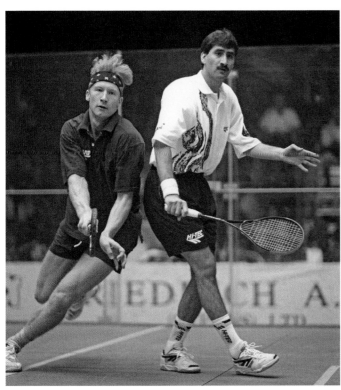

▲ Jansher in action against Del Harris in the 1995 World Open final.

Pakistan State Oil
World Open 1996

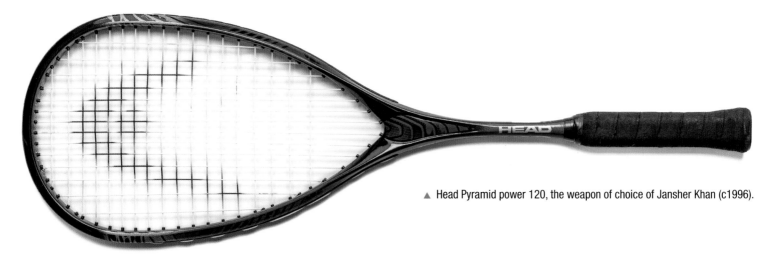

▲ Head Pyramid power 120, the weapon of choice of Jansher Khan (c1996).

Scoring/tin height/timing changes

DATE	SCORING	TIN HEIGHT	TIMES
Pre-1926	HiHo scoring to 15 points		
1923		Standardised at 19 inch/48 cm	
1926	HiHo scoring to 9 points introduced. Playing to 9 or 10 at 8-all (set 1 or 2)		
Pre-1989			1 minute max between all games except 2 minutes before 5th game
1989	Men's tour moves from HiHo to PAR 15	Men's Grand Prix (top tier) moves from 19 inch/48 cm to 17 inch/43 cm	Single serve introduced (faults not replayed). 90 seconds max between all games introduced
1993			90 seconds max between end of warm-up and match start introduced. 2 minutes between all games introduced for men's tour
2001	WSF adds PAR as alternative to HiHo for general play		
2004	Men's tour moves from PAR 15 to PAR 11		
2005		Men's tour (2* / PSA25) or higher moves to 17 inch/43 cm	
2008	Women's tour moves from HiHo to PAR 11		
2009	WSF makes PAR standard, and HiHo an alternative		
2011	PAR general play rules changed from 1 or 3 points at 14 all to 2 clear points		2 minutes between all games introduced for women's tour
2015		Women's tour moves to 17 inch/43cm	
2018			Warm-up max reduced from 5 mins to 4 mins
2021		Main tour moves entirely to 17 inch/43cm	

HiHo: *Hand in, Hand out (i.e. server only wins point when serving).*
PAR: *Point-A-Rally (every point counts, irrespective of serve).*

Courts worldwide

SQUASH PLAYING NATIONS & TOTAL SQUASH COURTS

AFRICA - 19 nations - 3842 courts

Botswana	50	Egypt	200	Ghana	6
Kenya	85	Lesotho	3	Malawi	5
Mauritius	2	Namibia	10	Nigeria	380
Seychelles	3	Sierra Leone	5	South Africa	2900
Sudan	15	Swaziland	2	Tanzania	6
Uganda	10	Zambia	40	Zaire	4
Zimbabwe	116				

ASIA - 27 nations - 3504 courts

Bahrain	60	Bangladesh	6	Brunei	10
China	28	Hong Kong	600	India	250
Indonesia	50	Iran	27	Iraq	20
Japan	60	Jordan	80	Kuwait	130
Korea	36	Lebanon	30	Macau	3
Malaysia	650	Muscat	20	Nepal	6
Oman	25	Pakistan	212	Philippines	35
Qatar	50	Saudi Arabia	180	Singapore	600
Sri Lanka	36	Thailand	50	UAE	250

EUROPE - 35 nations - 24117 courts

Andorra	25	Austria	595	Belgium	435
Bulgaria	3	Czech Republic	10	Cyprus	20
Croatia	1	Denmark	150	England	8831
Finland	690	France	1150	Germany	6135
Greece	14	Hungary	9	Iceland	3
Ireland	550	Israel	62	Italy	528
Latvia	2	Liechtenstein	5	Luxembourg	20
Malta	11	Monaco	6	Netherlands	1079
Norway	230	Poland	2	Portugal	100
Russia	5	Scotland	774	Slovenia	30
Spain	1200	Sweden	429	Switzerland	711
Turkey	2	Wales	300		

OCEANIA - 14 nations - 6794 courts

American Samoa	1	Australia	6000	Cook Islands	7
Fiji	10	Guam	2	New Caledonia	11
New Zealand	705	Norfolk Island	4	North Marianas	1
Papua N.Guinea	38	Tahiti	2	Tonga	2
Vanuatu	4	Western Samoa	7		

PAN AMERICA - 27 nations - 7424 courts

Antigua	2	Argentina	600	Bahamas	15
Barbados	14	Bermuda	10	Brazil	450
Canada	2090	Cayman Islands	5	Chile	50
Colombia	150	Costa Rica	10	Dominican Rep.	3
El Salavador	9	Ecuador	30	Guatemala	5
Guyana	3	Jamaica	15	Mexico	239
Panama	3	Paraguay	16	Peru	120
Uraguay	10	St. Lucia	2	St.Vincent	8
Trinidad	2	USA	3500	Venezuela	63

TOTAL NATIONS	122
WSF MEMBER NATIONS	97
TOTAL COURTS	45681

▲ This chart, produced by the WSF in 1993, indicated the worldwide spread of known courts at that point. It featured 122 nations in total (non-members in black), a number that expanded to 185 countries during the first two decades of the 21st century.

Malaysia

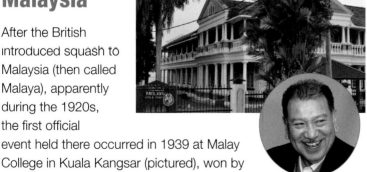

After the British introduced squash to Malaysia (then called Malaya), apparently during the 1920s, the first official event held there occurred in 1939 at Malay College in Kuala Kangsar (pictured), won by HRH Tuanku Ja'afar, ruler of the State of Negri Sembilan. Fast forward to 1973 the first national championship was won by YAM Tunku Imran – his son! Tunku Imran (pictured) went on to become an IOC member and President of the Commonwealth Games Federation, was instrumental in squash's first participation in the Commonwealth Games 1998 in his home country and was WSF President 1989-96.

Japan

The Japanese federation was founded in 1971, when the country, apart from a court at the British Embassy in Tokyo, had only three squash courts to play on, two in Yokohama and another in Kobe. When the JSM SuperSquash was held in Yokohama in 1995, it offered $200,000 combined. And far ahead of the push for parity, it was split equally between the men's and women's events.

Qatar

While there was a court in Qatar in the 1940s built by British oil industry workers, the establishment of squash at the Khalifa Centre in Doha in 1992 marked the beginning of Qatar as an international event host. Beginning with three courts it grew to nine in time to host the Asian Games squash event in 2006. In addition to the Qatar Classic which began in 1992, the venue has hosted five men's world titles, one women's and a men's World Junior championship to date.

Action from the memorable World Open 1998 final against Michelle Martin.

Fitz-Gerald's five

Sarah Fitz-Gerald and Michelle Martin vied for titles and top ranking throughout the 1990s. Twenty months younger than her Australian countrywoman Martin, Fitz-Gerald (born 1968) had won the World Junior title in 1987 before they then traded titles in the 1990s.

Martin won three World Open titles first (1993-95) with Fitz-Gerald taking the next three (1996-98), and carrying on with two more in 2001/02. But while she won 62 tour titles, it looked for a long while that Fitz-Gerald might not manage to include the British Open. Even after Martin won her last in 1998, New Zealander Leilani Joyce won it in 1999 and 2000, before 'Fitz' plugged the trophy gap with wins in 2001 and 2002.

Her third World title in Stuttgart 1998 was memorable for the way it was won. At 2-8 down in the deciding final game against Martin she recalled, *'At match ball, I remember telling myself to make the last point as difficult as possible. So I did; I relaxed and next thing I knew I earned a handout and a point'*. Points were added and after seven saved match balls she sensationally triumphed 10-9.

Fitz-Gerald confirms her number of World Open wins!

Australian teammates Fitz-Gerald and Liz Irving in 1994.

◄ Mentoring Nicol David was just one of Fitz-Gerald's roles.

The full set

Fitz-Gerald is the only player so far, male or female, to have won world titles at junior, senior and Masters level. And even after her tour retirement at the end of 2002 she returned as a member of the Australia Team in 2010 aged 41, where she was part of a winning team for the sixth time, eighteen years after the first.

Coldly focused on court, contrastingly warm off it, her trade-mark cut-off volley was a feature of her forceful, bustling game which started on its way via coaching from her three times (1956-58) Australian champion mother Judith (nee Tissot).

Her energy coupled with her engaging personality not only took her into coaching but serving on Boards, regionally, nationally and at world level. A squash star and a squash ambassador too.

Rodney's moment

On a November 1997 day in Petaling Jaya, Malaysia, Rodney Eyles, aged 30, produced the performance of his life to crush Peter Nicol 3-0 (15-11 15-12 15-12) in the final of the World Open. It was the only World Open final reached by the fast and often furiously focused Australian; but he had been in the British Open final the year before while ranked two in the world, where he was thwarted by Jansher Khan. Earlier, in 1991, Eyles had been a member of the Australian World Team championship winning squad.

▲ Rodney Eyles beating Peter Nicol in the 1997 World Open final.

A double hander

Double-handed players are common in tennis, but the only squash player to play this way at the highest level was Peter Marshall. It was thought that he would grow out of it but he did not. People wondered whether it would be damaging for his spine, or that it may affect his reach. The fact that he reached number two in the world during 1994/95 suggests not.

World champions in 1999

On the eve of the semi-finals, the four players contesting the women's World Open 1999 in Seattle, USA, celebrated with Heather McKay who was inducted into the WISPA (women's tour) Hall of Fame.

This took place before Cassie Jackman (ENG) went on to win, beating Michelle Martin in the final (pictured). Left to right: Jackman, Leilani Joyce, McKay, Natalie Grainger, Martin.

◄ Marshall demonstrating his action against Australian Anthony Hill at the British Open 1994.

THE YOUNG MEN WHO HAVE REACHED THE PINNACLE –
SQUASH'S WORLD JUNIOR CHAMPIONS

1980
PETER NANCE
Australia

1982
SOHAIL QAISER
Pakistan

1984
CHRIS ROBERTSON
Australia

1986
JANSHER KHAN
Pakistan

1988
DEL HARRIS
England

1990
SIMON PARKE
England

1992
JUHA RAUMOLIN
Finland

1994
AHMED BARADA
Egypt

1996
AHMED FAIZY
Egypt

1998
ONG BENG HEE
Malaysia

2000
KARIM DARWISH
Egypt

2002
JAMES WILLSTROP
England

2004.2006
RAMY ASHOUR
Egypt

2008.2009
MOHAMED ELSHORBAGY
Egypt

2010
AMR KHALED KHALIFA
Egypt

2011.2012
MARWAN ELSHORBAGY
Egypt

2013
KARIM EL HAMMAMY
Egypt

2014.2015
DIEGO ELIAS
Peru

2016
EAIN YOW NG
Malaysia

2017
MARWAN TAREK
Egypt

2018.2019
MOSTAFA ASAL
Egypt

2022
ROWAN DAMMING
Netherlands

2023
HAMZA KHAN
Pakistan

2024
MOHAMAD ZAKARIA
Egypt

www.squashlibrary.info
info@squashlibrary.info

Squash archive and
information resource

Most photos kindly provided by Steve Line

Getting into Games

In a three-year period, squash joined the programme of the four major multi-sport Games set below the Olympics. First, in 1995, the Pan American Games introduced squash in Mar del Plata in Argentina. Then the World

Games ('the Olympics for non-Olympic sports') included squash in the 1997 edition in Lahti, Finland. The quartet was completed in 1998 when squash became part of the Asian Games in Bangkok, Thailand and the Commonwealth Games staged in Kuala Lumpur, Malaysia.

REGIONAL GAMES / CHAMPIONSHIPS BEGIN

REGION	START	EVENT
	2003	African Games
	1996	African Team championships (a)
	1998	Asian Games
	1981	Asian Team championships (b)
		European Games
	1973	European Team championships (c)
	1995	Pan American Games
	1993	Pan American Team championships
	1979	Oceania (Pacific) Games
	1993	Oceania Team championships

(a) Women's from 2011 • (b) Women's from 1986 • (c) Women's from 1978
NOTE: Games = Multi-Sport, Championships = Squash alone

FIRST SQUASH 'MAJOR GAMES' CHAMPIONS

	MEN'S	WOMEN'S	M/W TEAMS	MEN'S DOUBLES	WOMEN'S DOUBLES	MIXED DOUBLES
PanAm Games 1995	Gary Waite (CAN)	Heather Wallace (CAN)	Canada / Canada			
World Games 1997	Ahmed Barada (EGY)	Sarah Fitz-Gerald (AUS)				
Asian Games 1998	Zarak Jahan Khan (PAK)	Nicol David (MAS)				
Commonwealth Games 1998	Peter Nicol (SCO)	Michelle Martin (AUS)		Mark Chaloner & Paul Johnson (ENG)	Cassie Jackman & Sue Wright (ENG)	Michelle Martin & Craig Rowland (AUS)

Reaching the summit

For the first two decades of men's rankings, only the Asia and Oceania regions had men holding the number one spot. It was not until 1998 that Europe first planted their flag at the peak, Pan America a year later: Peter Nicol (Scotland/England) and Jonathon Power (Canada) being the first to do so; within PanAm the first South American would become Diego Elias who took top spot in 2023. The first African world number one was Egyptian male Amr Shabana, who reached the ranking summit in April 2006.

The women's peak had been claimed by Australian, English and New Zealand players for the first twenty ranking years before Natalie Pohrer (Grainger), representing USA, was in top spot for one month in June 2003. Then, beginning in January 2006, Asia dominated until 2015 in the person of Malaysian Nicol David, who after an initial three-month stint, added an unbroken nine years and one month. Next came the African continent via Egyptians, starting with Raneem El Welily who took over from David in September 2015 and managed two periods totaling 23 months.

top (l/r)
Peter Nicol
Jonathon Power
middle (l/r)
Natalie Grainger
Nicol David
bottom (l/r)
Amr Shabana
Raneem El Welily

Double dealing

In the early days of squash in England, on unregulated courts, doubles is also known to have been played locally. After the standardisation of squash there were only a few larger doubles courts built in the UK, notably during the 1930s, and these were soon taken down again. After that, squash doubles, if played at all, was on singles courts. The real start for the international (softball) doubles game can be said to have been in 1988, when two wider doubles courts were constructed at the RAC Woodcote Park clubhouse, situated south of London.

They happened to be 7.62m (25ft) wide, their length the same as a singles court. The WSF decided to approve this as the standard doubles size in 1992. The advent of portable courts with movable side-walls encouraged the WSF to start the World Doubles championship in Hong Kong, China in 1997. This was almost immediately followed by doubles featuring as part of squash's debut in the Commonwealth Games in Kuala Lumpur in 1998 (pictured). Soon though, it was felt that the rallies at elite level needed to be shortened, so leading to the increased competition court width agreed in 2008. Later the doubles tin height was lowered to 13in/33cm in 2012.

SQUASH COURTS (LENGTH 9.75m /32ft)	COURT WIDTH
Singles court	6.40m /21ft
1992 WSF Doubles court for general play	7.62m /25ft
2008 WSF Doubles court for international competition	8.42m /27ft 6in
2012 Tin height for international competition doubles courts reduced to 33cm /13in	

Hardball doubles
North America, unlike England, had a long tradition in doubles squash, played with the hardball on larger (both longer and wider) courts, specifically built for the doubles game. It began at the Racquet Club of Philadelphia in 1907 and was standardised by the US Squash Association prior to the first national doubles championships in 1933. A pro tour began in the 1970s; and since 1981 the World Hardball Doubles championships have been held, though not always at regular intervals, the most recent to date in 2017.

Hardball singles

Although hardball singles withered through the 1990s, Ohio born Mark Talbott (pictured) dominated the genre in a career that began in 1980 until his retirement in 1996. Over the period he won 116 events including majors many times over. During this time many North American squash courts were converted to the international softball game.

▲ A new squash magazine in the USA was Squash News, launched in 1978. Within a year it became the US federation official magazine, and continued until the baton was taken up by Squash Magazine which began in 1997. Here are the first Squash News and Squash Magazine covers.

Rankings go monthly

World rankings were published every two months until the player associations decided that the number of events on their calendars merited monthly rankings. That point came in February 1998 for the men and February 2001 for women. The first are shown, the men's monthly list featuring Peter Nicol's debut at number one.

WISPA WOMEN'S Feb-01		PSA MEN'S Feb-98	
1 Leilani Joyce	NZL	1 Peter Nicol	SCO
2 Carol Owens	AUS	2 Jansher Khan	PAK
3 Sarah Fitz-Gerald	AUS	3 Jonathon Power	CAN
4 Linda Charman	ENG	4 Rodney Eyles	AUS
5 Natalie Grainger	ENG	5 Ahmed Barada	EGY
6 Tania Bailey	ENG	6 Simon Parke	ENG
7 Suzanne Horner	ENG	7 Alex Gough	WAL
8 Fiona Geaves	ENG	8 Anthony Hill	AUS
9 Stephanie Brind	ENG	9 Del Harris	ENG
10 Rachael Grinham	AUS	10 Dan Jenson	AUS
11 Vanessa Atkinson	NED	11 Mark Chaloner	ENG
12 Cassie Campion	ENG	12 Peter Marshall	ENG
13 Rebecca Macree	ENG	13 Chris Walker	ENG
14 Sabine Schoene	GER	14 Paul Johnson	ENG
15 Sue Wright	ENG	15 Mark Cairns	ENG
16 Jenny Tranfield	ENG	16 Byron Davis	AUS
17 Pamela Nimmo	SCO	17 Martin Heath	SCO
18 Vicky Botwright	ENG	18 Derek Ryan	IRL
19 Maha Zein	EGY	19 Amir Wagih	EGY
20 Natalie Grinham	AUS	20 Julien Bonetat	FRA

Nationalities listed are as at the ranking list date.

Eady's choice

Welshman Roger Eady became the first paid executive director of the ISRF (International Squash Rackets Federation) in 1983, while also taking on the role of secretary of ISPA (International Squash Players Association) the following year. But by 1989 it became clear that both federations needed their own head, and Eady chose PSA, where he stayed until 1994.

WORLD TOP 10 PLAYERS – BY NATION

Country	July 1983		July 1993		July 2003		July 2013		July 2023	
	Men	Women	Men	Women	Men	Women	Men	Women	Men	Women
Australia	2	3	5	4	3	2		1		
Belgium										1
Canada				1	1					
Egypt	1				1		5	1	5	5
England	3	5	3	4	2	5	3	3	1	1
France					1		1		1	
Germany				1						
Ireland								1		
Malaysia					1			2		
Netherlands						1	1			
New Zealand	2	2	1			1		1	1	1
Pakistan	2		1							
Peru									1	
Scotland					1					
Spain							1			
USA						1				2
Wales								1		

Shuffling the initials

25 years after it began, the world federation (ISRF) changed its name in 1992 and became the WSF. It was part of a trend where the *rackets* was dropped from *squash rackets* as the name of the sport.

Meanwhile, the men's player association (ISPA) merged with their hardball cousins WPSA, the North American pro body, leading to the new name: PSA, introduced from January 1993. (Hardball singles had discontinued, but the hardball doubles group split away again in 2000 to form ISDA (International Squash Doubles Association).

The Women's player body, WISPA, changed its name briefly in 2012 to WSA (Women's Squash Association) before merging with the men's PSA from January 2015.

1. Millenium Park, Chicago (2009)

2. Krakow, Poland (2015)

3. The Bund, Shanghai (2004)

4. Marriott Hotel island, Hurghada, Egypt (1998)

5. Hong Kong Harbour (2005)

6. Luxor, Egypt (2010)

7. Seoul Plaza, Korea (2009)

Courts move outside

Show courts had arrived in the previous decade, but it was in the 1990s that inspired locations first began to appear. The most iconic was the court placed near the Pyramids of Giza (see page 168), which was first used in 1996 and saw its photo splashed around the world. Egypt followed this two years later by building a court on the island bar of the Marriott Hotel in Hurghada, reachable by a wooden walkway. Other stunning sites followed all over the world inspired by them.

CHAPTER 10

SQUASH IN THE 2000s

The start of the new millennium saw world titles being won by players from a greater variety of nations. Nicol David from Malaysia became dominant over the women's chasing pack in the second half of the decade. The Egyptian male take-over of the top order was beginning, spearheaded by Amr Shabana; while the widening international spread of elite players and squash generally was continuing.

David under pressure from Natalie Grinham.

SQUASH IN THE 2000s
David takes centre stage

Kuala Lumpur was awarded the 1998 Commonwealth Games and squash was added to the programme. This galvanised the Malaysian Squash Federation. Development programmes were initiated - which paid dividends with several high fliers being nurtured, including Ong Beng Hee. But none was more successful than a young girl from the island of Penang: Nicol David. Her potential was so well recognised that David (born 1983) was added to the squad to expose her to the Games; and only a year later in July 1999, she won her first World Junior title aged just 15.

Needing a game-changer

That hers would become a stellar career may have not seemed so likely as she emerged from the junior ranks. Athletic, fast, and a superb retriever, she needed more components to compete as an adult. As she expressed it, *'I was having trouble adjusting to the transition from junior to senior squash and I was becoming very frustrated. I needed to find a game changer.'*

A move from Malaysia to Amsterdam was decided upon, and while it was not easy being a young adult far from home, coming under the wing of Australian coach Liz Irving there proved immensely successful. Irving added volleying and court craft to turn the compact so-called 'Duracell Bunny' with an engaging wide smile into a formidable force.

◄ David with Liz Irving, her long-time coach from Australia. Irving had herself been runner up in one World Open and three British Open finals between 1988 and 1995. After her retirement she became a highly successful coach.

David playing Vicky Botwright in the 2008 World Open final.

◄ Prince O3 Tour (c2005) the racket of choice of Nicol David and Peter Nicol.

'My strengths are my endurance, fitness, pace and agility on court, and these contributed to my retaining the top position for such a long time. I was able to keep my opponents under pressure.' is how David summed herself up.

These traits were very much the case, but so was a steely determination. So often she would be loose and go behind in a game, only to focus, tighten up and take it. There would be no better illustration of this than the Women's World championship final in Cairo in December 2014. Opponent Raneem El Welily was 2/1 ahead in games and at 10-6 up in the fourth, only a point away from winning. David saved four match balls to level the match, and then went on to take her eighth title.

Recognition

Accolades and awards were sprinkled on her. Asian Sportswoman of the year 2007 was one; another was Malaysian 'Datukship' (a dame-type title for which she was the youngest ever recipient). These not only recognised her on-court success but also her humility and ambassadorship for her country and squash.

► Aged 13, David was awarded a place in the qualification draw of the 1996 Women's World Open. While she did not make the main draw David did get to meet three-time winner Michelle Martin.

Four-timer Omneya

Egyptian player Omneya Abdel Kawy is the only player to have represented her country four times in the World Junior Team championship – at a time when it was only held every two years. She did so in 1997/99/01/03, the start of the first being just before her 12th birthday. She played 23 team matches in the four editions losing only once to Nicol David - and her team won the 1999 and 2003 events. She ended her junior career winning the individual event too, in 2003. As a senior she rose as high as four in the world in 2010, the year she was runner up in the World Open, losing the final to Nicol David.

Top and bottom

The WISPA (women's tour) promotional visits ran from 1999 until 2009 to 27 worldwide places, followed by WSF Ambassador visits from 2011 to 2019 which added another 14 – many of which featured Nicol David. She would go on court with a procession of local players from top men and women to juniors, take part in clinics and charm the media who were being encouraged to cover squash.

Every continent was covered, and WISPA included the most northerly squash court in the world at Longyearbyen on the Svalbard archipelago in the Arctic Circle in 2006. The following year saw David, Sarah Fitz-Gerald and Rachael Grinham at Ushuaia on Tierra del Fuego, the southernmost tip of South America, at the world's most southerly court at the Las Hayas hotel in the town (along with Buenos Aires, Montevideo and Santiago).

1. Nicol David and Sarah Fitz-Gerald showed the WISPA flag to huskies on Svalbard.

2. The Las Hayas court, the most southern in the world, had a sloping roof that disallowed lobbing.

3. WISPA/WSF programmes sponsor lost on Svalbard, waving for help!

4. Rachael Grinham and Nicol David visited the Great Wall of China during their 2004 visit, managing to get squash introduced on Chinese National TV during their promotional trip.

Carla joins dynasty

When London based Carla Khan won the El Salvador Open in 2002 she became the first Pakistani female to win a tour title. The granddaughter of four times British Open winner Azam Khan who herself won five tour titles and reached 21 in the world rankings in 2004 became another member of the 'Khan Dynasty' of champions.

MEN'S / WOMEN'S TOUR MEMBERSHIP

1977 - 2023 • Total membership and the nations represented

YEAR	MEN		WOMEN	
	MEMBERS	NATIONS	MEMBERS	NATIONS
2023	897	67	461	59
2013	445	58	243	46
2003	290	40	121	40
1993	267	41	81	21
1983	97	14	30*	6
1977	34	6		

July ranking lists used • *Tour formation year, pre-1st AGM

Power v Nicol

The first half of the decade saw Peter Nicol dominating the top-spot of the world rankings, amassing 60 months there in total; while Canadian Jonathon Power, the first Pan American to reach the number one position, held it for 14 months. However, neither player managed to win another World Open title during the period; although it should be noted that their opportunities were limited as it did not take place in 2000 and 2001. So, one world title each in total, Power in 1998, Nicol the following year. The two players swapped the order at the British Open: Nicol winning the crown in 1998 and Power in 1999; with Nicol adding a second in 2002.

Nicol was very much the opposite of Power. Not simply that he was a left hander, happy to play conservatively, and generally reserved. In contrast, Power was volatile and loved nothing better than attacking with feints and winner attempts. Nicol would impress with quiet durability while Power was an argumentative crowd pleaser.

The world title was shared by four other players in the decade. David Palmer (2002/06), Thierry Lincou (2004), and Egyptians Amr Shabana (2003/05/07/09) and Ramy Ashour (2008, plus later in 2012/14).

Power executes flamboyantly against Nicol!

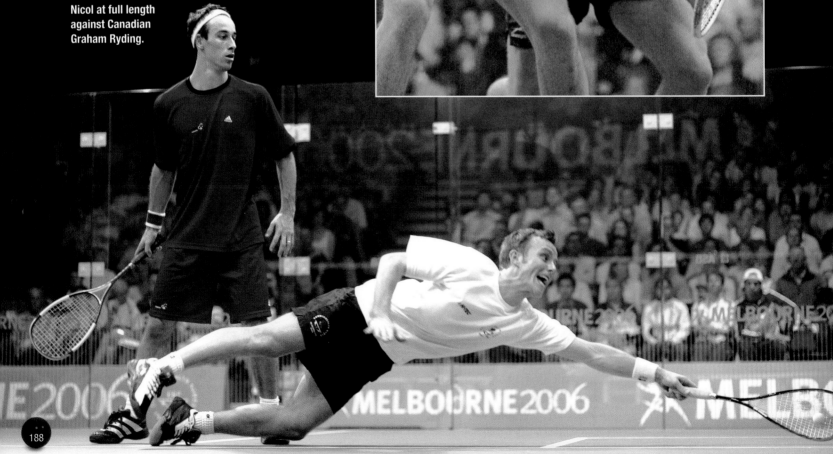

Nicol at full length against Canadian Graham Ryding.

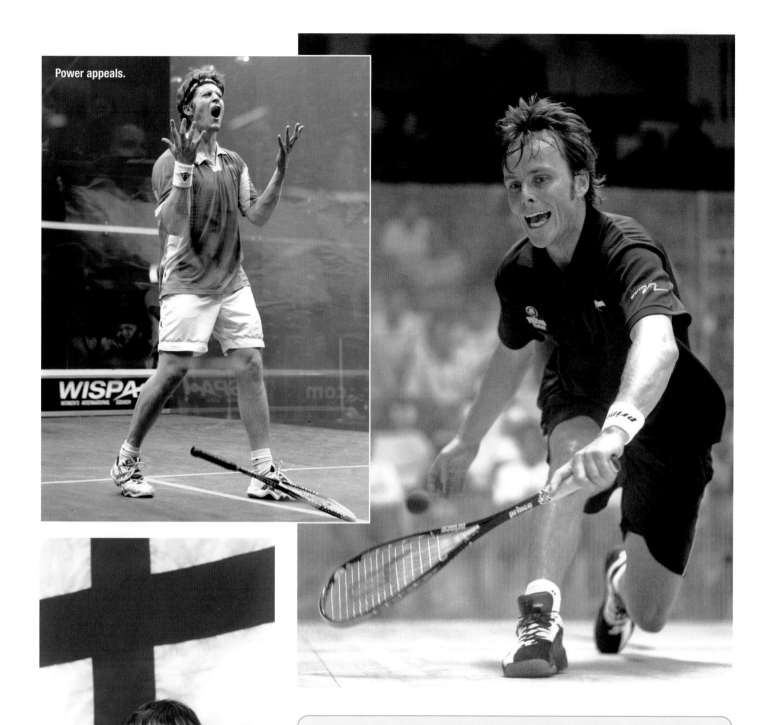

Power appeals.

Nicol changed allegiance from Scotland to England in 2001 to take advantage of more support in the country in which he was based.

The unfinished Scottish British Open

The only unfinished British Open final took place in Aberdeen in 1999, when locally born player Peter Nicol was unable to defend his title. He won the first game against Canadian Jonathon Power 17-15, lost the second 12-15, and then was forced to retire before passing out with the effects of enteritis and accompanying dehydration (pictured left). Early rounds had taken place at Aberdeen Squash Club, the first in Scotland and one of the oldest squash clubs in the world. Opening in 1913, while the courts were destroyed during WW2, they were soon rebuilt.

1999 BRITISH OPEN SQUASH CHAMPIONSHIPS

Amr Shabana

All over the place

Amr Shabana (born 1979) was initially very much the opposite of Nicol. Mercurial and inconsistent, expressive and humorous; it seemed that the Cairo left-hander may not fulfil his obvious potential. The early part of his career saw him 'all over the place.' Flurries of winners laced with a flow of unforced errors and distracting expressive outbursts were his trademark.

He had been a part of the first Egyptian men's team to win the world title in 1999, but it was not until December 2003 that the 24-year-old Shabana's growing maturity really showed - when he won the World Open in Lahore, Pakistan as lowly ninth seed.

He had not only begun to straighten-up his demeanour and consistency, but his game too. Fewer loose angles for his opponent to feed off. By April 2006 he had taken the world number one ranking, and didn't relinquish it for 33 months. Strangely though, Shabana did not win the British Open. However, only two men, the legends that were Jahangir and Jansher Khan, have won more World Open championships than Shabana's four (2003/05/07/09).

▲ Shabana and David together on the cover of a squash annual. When the World Opens were played together for the first time in 2005, Shabana won the men's, David took the women's title.

▲ Shabana's signature racket, the Dunlop I.C.E. custom elite (c2006), with its unusual interchangeable grip, for altering the weight balance of the racket.

Going his own way

David Palmer, the most successful Australian male since Geoff Hunt, may not have been the most artful or best mover amongst his peers but he built up his game, adding volleying and pressure to his defensive qualities. Nicknamed 'the Marine,' he was tough, abrasive, and quite simply very difficult to beat. Palmer was strong-minded too. Not for him was the AIS (Australian Institute of Sport), but instead developing independent relationships with coaches Joe Shaw and later Shaun Moxham away from his home country.

In addition to his two World Open wins (2002/06), he was a member of two Australian world champion teams (2001/03), a four-time British Open champion (2001/03/04/08), and was world number one for five months between 2001 and 2006.

Palmer in the front corner against Amr Shabana.

▲ Palmer played Egyptian Karim Darwish (foreground) in the 2008 World Open. Darwish would rise to world number one for 11 months in 2009/10.

Super speedy White

Palmer beat John White (right) in the World Open 2002 final, a year in which White, Australian born but Scottish representing, also reached the British Open final. For two months in 2004 (March/April), White held world number one spot. White was one of the hardest hitters ever in squash, the ball reaching speeds of up to 172 miles per hour.

Five-sided glass

The first time a five-sided glass court was used was at the women's Qatar Airways Challenge in Hyderabad, India in 2006 when ASB added a glass floor to their showcourt. It had raised dots for grip, a sprung underfloor which could be any colour, and many tiny LED lights so that names, scores and boxes could be illuminated.

▲ ASB court company founder Horst Babinsky inspects the glass floor in Hyderabad.

Hover-court!

For the 2002 Commonwealth Games in Manchester and subsequent events there, the showcourt in the newly built English National Squash Centre needed to move through a removable wall into the adjacent indoor athletics area where 2,500 seats would be erected. This was achieved by building the court on an elevated base complete with hydraulics so that it could slide across for major events.

Squash Info data cache

Peter Nicol was the first player inputted into Squash's international information database, www.squashinfo.com. Started in 2004 by Howard Harding (pictured below), by 2024 it was providing access to leading players' career records and results of significant events back to the 1960s with a cache comprising more than 250,000 matches in over 10,000 events, played by 20,000 players.

Squash Info
the definitive squash resource

Snapping the action

Steve Line (right), along with Fritz Borchert, have enduringly provided photos for media. While it started out as being for newspapers and publications, electronic media added greatly to the landscape. Borchert retired after 30 snapping years, while Line (also pictured in work mode) currently has 40 years under his belt – with a selection of his superb work enlivening this book. They, Steve Cubbins and many nationally based photographers and website operators, have played an important specialist role for the sport.

Internet live

In 2004, 25 February that year to be exact, the first live streaming of a pro squash event took place at the semi-finals of the Tournament of Champions in New York. Peter Nicol and Jonathon Power were the first two players who could be watched in this way, followed by John White and Lee Beachill – and 200 viewers did.

New scoring

When Frenchman Thierry Lincou beat Nick Matthew in the final of the Hong Kong Open 2004 he had the distinction of becoming the first player to win an event using PAR11. The scoring to 15 was dropped from September 2004 after a trial at the non-points scoring Super Series Finals. In 2008 the women's tour moved to PAR 11 too.

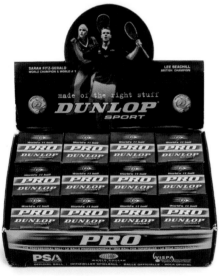

▲ Dunlop double yellow dot squash balls (c2005), endorsed by Sarah Fitz-Gerald and Lee Beachill.

Another look

Video reviews came to squash in March 2005 at the men's Canary Wharf Classic in London. Match referees, but not players yet, could ask for video replays. After testing during early rounds the project went live for the semis and final.

▲ SQ050 racket launched by Neoxxline (c2004), along with their lawn tennis rackets line. The squash version was actually illegal to play with. Not only because it was asymmetrical, but also because the strung area exceeded the maximum, it being 516 cm2, a number they even printed on the frame!

PSA MEN'S RANKING – DEC 2004	
1 Lee Beachill (ENG)	(Oct 2004)
2 Thierry Lincou (FRA)	(Jan 2004)
3 Peter Nicol (ENG)	(Feb 1998)
4 David Palmer (AUS)	(Sep 2001)
5 Amr Shabana (EGY)	(Apr 2006)
6 John White (SCO)	(Mar 2004)
7 Nick Matthew (ENG)	(Jun 2010)
8 Karim Darwish (EGY)	(Jan 2009)
9 Jonathon Power (CAN)	(May 1999)
10 Gregory Gaultier (FRA)	(Nov 2009)

The December 2004 Men's World Top 10 was remarkable as every single player in it had been, or would become, world number one. The dates they reached top spot are in brackets (with Nicol still representing Scotland at that point).

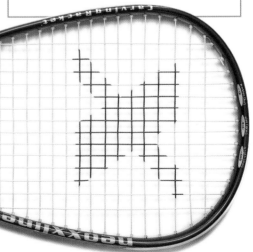

Large nations, small squash beginnings

Squash was played by the British in Shanghai, Beijing and Hong Kong before WW2; but the real start of squash in China was much later, when two courts were built at the White Swan Hotel in Guangzhou c1984. More courts followed in hotels and embassies before being added to residential developments; and clubs began to appear, fuelled by arrivals from Hong Kong and internationally. This photo was taken when the Chinese Federation was formed in 2004.

In Russia in Moscow there was a squash court at the Indian embassy (pictured). Then, in 1987 Muscovites could begin to play on a court at Club Prometey, followed by public courts in Moscow, Krasnoyarsk and St Petersburg.

Downsizing

To provide an entry route into squash for younger children, it was recognised by England Squash that a shorter racket and a more suitable large ball would be needed. To accomplish this Mini Squash was introduced in 2003 on a national children's TV programme in UK, demonstrated by Peter Nicol. Since the start with inflatable courts, backboards and other hitting surfaces have been developed too.

NATIONAL FEDERATION FOUNDING DATES

Afghanistan	INS	D R of Congo	2008	Indonesia	1979	Mexico	1968	St Vincent & Gren	1979
Andorra	1984	Cook Islands	1992	Iraq	1986	Monaco	1969	Saudi Arabia	1992
Argentina	1983	Cyprus	1983	Ireland	1935	Mongolia	2010	Scotland	1936
Armenia	2011	Czech Republic	1992	Isle of Man	1980	Myanmar	INS	Serbia	2001
Austria	1978	Denmark	1971	Israel	1982	Namibia	1974	Singapore	1970
Australia	1934	Ecuador	INS	Italy	1985	Nepal	1988	Slovakia	1993
Bahamas	1971	Egypt	1931	Jamaica	1977	Netherlands	1938	Slovenia	1992
Bahrain	1982	El Salvador	INS	Japan	1971	New Caledonia	1987	South Africa	1910
Bangladesh	1978	England	1928	Jersey	1949	New Zealand	1932	Spain	1974
Barbados	1978	Estonia	1997	Jordan	1980	Nigeria	1974	Sri Lanka	1981
Belarus	2006	Fiji	1968	Kenya	1952	Norway	1978	Sweden	1965
Belgium	1974	Finland	1971	Korea	1989	Pakistan	1954	Switzerland	1973
Bermuda	1959	France	1974	Kuwait	1968	Palestine	INS	Tahiti	2013
Bolivia	2014	Guatemala	1993	Latvia	1999	Panama	1998	Thailand	1979
Botswana	INS	Germany	1973	Lebanon	1987	Papua New Guinea	1977	Trinidad & Tobago	1977
Brazil	1991	Gibraltar	1993	Libya	2020	Paraguay	1994	Turkey	2003
British Virgin Is	1992	Greece	1974	Liechtenstein	1988	Peru	1970	Uganda	1972
Bulgaria	INS	Guernsey	2002	Lithuania	2000	Philippines	1974	Ukraine	2004
Canada*	1915	Guyana	1997	Luxembourg	1975	Poland	2002	USA*	1904
Cayman Islands	2007	Hong Kong, China	1961	Macau	1987	Portugal	1985	Vanuatu	2009
Chile	2002	Hungary	1989	Malawi	1970	Qatar	1984	Venezuela	1998
China	2004	Iceland	1988	Malaysia	1972	Romania	2014	Wales	1938
Chinese Taipei	1995	India	1953	Malta	1983	Russia	1990	Zambia	1964
Colombia	1988	Iran	1972	Mauritius	1978	Samoa	1979	Zimbabwe	1952

*Primarily hardball & international matches until softball courts began to emerge from the 1970s. INS: Information not supplied.

Two from Toowoomba

Toowoomba in Queensland is the Australian city from where the Grinham sisters emerged. Both small and slight, older Rachael with a unique unorthodox style, and Natalie, arguably the fastest player of her time. Rachael used her trademark floaty lobs, deft flicks and drops to wristily win the 1993 World Juniors; and in 2007 add the World Open crown – beating Natalie in the final. Both moved out of Australia to be closer to tour venues, Rachael, typically not doing the obvious, so to Cairo rather than Europe. Natalie settled in Netherlands, and in 2008 changed her allegiance to that country.

From her Egyptian base, Rachael also won four British Open titles (2003/04/07/09), the 2007 edition being memorable for her final comeback from 2-0 down to Nicol David in an 87-minute final. She recorded 16 months at World number one beginning in August 2004.

▲ Sisterly battle with Natalie in front.

Commonwealth success

This was not possible for younger Natalie as David was now blocking her way, so she had to settle for 29 months in second spot. Natalie reached four World Open finals (2004/06/07/09) but coming away with only silver medals. Gold was hers at the Commonwealth Games in 2006 though, when she scooped all three on offer; winning the singles, women's and mixed doubles. Rachael has the other Commonwealth squash record – holding eight, the greatest number of squash medals. Rachael also holds the title of oldest women's tour winner, taking the 2021 Australian Open title aged 44.

▲ Natalie shows off her three Commonwealth golds.

▲ Rachael Grinham.

NZ bred & NZ adopted

In the space of four years New Zealander Leilani Joyce (nee Marsh, later Rorani) managed to win titles, medals and retire in a short but spectacular career. Hard running, hard hitting and being unflappable under pressure took her to two British Open titles, in 1999 and 2000. She was also runner up in the 2000 World Open (to Carol Owens) and in 2001 (to Sarah Fitz-Gerald).

From November 2000 she was ranked as world number one for 11 months. Then in December 2001 she suffered a complete tear of her Achilles tendon. Battling back she made it to the Commonwealth Games in August 2002. Rusty, but she won golds in both the Women's Doubles with Carol Owens, and Mixed Doubles with Glen Wilson.

Carol Owens playing Natalie Grainger (left).

Leilani Joyce.

Crossing the Tasman

Before becoming a successful Kiwi, Carol Owens had been an outstanding Aussie. She was a member of three Australian World Team winning teams (1994/96/98) and in 2000 had won her first (of two) World Open titles. Disenchanted with her national support, she declined to represent Australia any longer, and having already moved from Melbourne to New Zealand she changed allegiance. For NZ she won Commonwealth doubles gold (with Joyce) and also the silver singles medal in 2002.

Owens won the World Open twice.

A strong athlete, she had great movement but inexplicable lapses too. A slew of errors could interrupt a thread of solid play, but Owens was always a fighter. At the end of a period of 127 months in the world top ten that had begun in July 1993 she won her second World Open in December 2003, and decided to retire at that point at the age of 32, saying that she felt that holding both the title and number one spot simultaneously meant that her ambitions were fulfilled.

First Europeans

In a strange quirk of timing the first world champions from the European mainland were crowned a week apart in December 2004. They both won it once, and also happened to have been born just a month apart in 1976. First came Frenchman Thierry Lincou born on the Indian Ocean island of Réunion. He won his in Qatar, beating Lee Beachill in the final; while English-born Vanessa Atkinson who had moved to Netherlands aged ten won in Kuala Lumpur. There, she beat Natalie Grinham in the final, the Australian who would later become a Dutch teammate.

The similarities stopped on court, though. While Lincou in his distinctive knee-length socks used his strength based around a hard training regime to look to maintain control of the court, keeping the ball tight; that was not the Atkinson way. She was more of an instinctive attacker, always looking for opportunities to open up the rally, sometimes showing her emotions on court too, unlike quiet and undramatic Lincou. Each in their own style topped the world rankings, Lincou for 14 months, Atkinson for five.

Atkinson in action.

▲ Atkinson poses with the World Open trophy.

▲ Lincou celebrates against Lee Beachill, the Englishman who was world number one for three months in 2004/05.

A world day

The 9/11 Twin Towers atrocity took place in New York as qualification was getting underway for the 2001 US Open. The event was postponed and subsequently played the following January. That month also saw the start of the annual World Squash Day, initially to remember those who died but also to support the game. It took

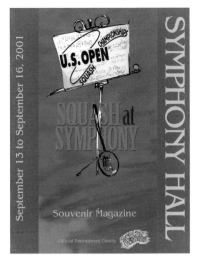

▲ The originally scheduled 2001 US Open.

place at Lambs Club, London comprising an eight player pro-event alongside a 15-a-side New York v London match, before developing into an international annual promotional day.

▲ From left top liners Peter Nicol (1st), Paul Price (4th) and Peter Marshall (7th) were amongst those who took part at Lambs.

Lambs lost

Lambs Club in the City of London, the first World Squash Day host, had been internationally known as host of the early rounds of the British Open (1989 – 94) as well as the British Junior Open. The nine-court facility was the largest in London before closing in 2007 to make way for apartments.

Urban squash

The start of Urban Squash programmes in the USA was in 1996. Founded by former squash pro Greg Zaff, SquashBusters in Boston set out to introduce squash to young people in urban public schools; and so broaden their access to opportunities, and improve their health and fitness. Seven years later in 2003 it partnered Northeastern University (pic) to build the first urban youth centre to combine classrooms and courts.

Other cities began to take up the baton and in 2005 NUSEA (National Urban Squash and Education Association) was formed to coordinate the city programmes, which in 2017 changed its name to SEA (Squash and Education Alliance) as overseas initiatives also began to join. Meanwhile, in 2007 the USSRA changed its name to US Squash, as part of a worldwide trend to drop rackets from the name of the sport.

CHAPTER 11

SQUASH IN THE 2010s & 2020s

As the squash story reaches the present day, ranking domination and sport presentation have seen major shifts. Many Egyptians are taking the prime slots in the rankings, like Ramy Ashour and Ali Farag; but more non-traditional nations, including from South America, are also coming to the fore. The women's game is for a large part dominated by Nour El Sherbini. The introduction of SQUASHTV has taken squash into the broadcast mainstream. Looking forward, the inclusion of squash in the 2028 Olympic Games will be a great boost for the game and its further development.

Ashour has Nick Matthew in trouble.

SQUASH IN THE 2010s & 2020s

Ashour, assured but...

If Ramy Ashour had more trustworthy knees and hamstrings who knows how much more successful the Egyptian might have become. As it is, he had a sparkling career in which he became the youngest male winner of the World Junior title in 2004, aged 16. It was one he retained when it was next played in 2006, the first male to do so.

Other milestones were swept up in the following years. Three World Open titles (2008/12/14); 40 tour titles; becoming the first Egyptian to win the British Open for 48 years in 2013; and 21 months at world number one between 2010 and 2013. All these managed between extensive injury time-outs, along with reaching two more World championship finals, in 2009 and again in 2016 when he had to retire in the fourth game against Karim Abdel Gawad.

Oozing with talent

Ashour, nicknamed 'the Artist,' oozed with talent on court and personality off it. A couple of paces further up the court than almost anybody else, with a short backswing he would cut off the ball and decrease his opponent's reaction time. A volley drop, a tight drive or something even more creative would leave an opponent floundering. Smiles and a humorous or enigmatic comment would often punctuate play.

▲ Ashour in control against James Willstrop.

◀ Ashour with the World championship trophy in 2012. It was the second of his three World Open titles.

David still dominates

Nicol David continued to dominate the rankings and top titles as the second decade of the 2000s unfolded, her last major being Asian Games gold in 2018 on her 35th birthday, before initiating 'the Nicol David Foundation', a charity programme to support girls squash and education in Malaysia. The Malaysian won 81 tour titles, including eight World Open and five British Open crowns; and maintained her world number one status for a record-breaking 109 consecutive months from August 2006 to August 2015. As fellow world champion Amr Shabana summed up, *'She has laid down a benchmark – legendary demeanor, razor-sharp attitude, focused and professional'.* A legend of the sport, enough said!

▲ Nicol David battling with Jenny Duncalf (left) from England, who was runner up to David in the 2011 World Open final.

Fitz-Gerald's full house

Five players – all from Oceania – have won World Masters titles to add to their World Opens (WO) - including just one man, Ross Norman. Of these, only Sarah Fitz-Gerald (pic) has also won the World Junior Individual (WJ) title to complete the set. The group, with their World Open win years in brackets and Masters age group win dates:

Vicki Cardwell (AUS), WO-1983 + O35-1990, O45-2001, O55-2010

Sarah Fitz-Gerald (AUS), WO-1996/97/98/01/02 + WJ-1987, O35-2006, O45-2014/16/18

Michelle Martin (AUS), WO-1993/94/95 + O45-2012

Heather McKay (AUS). WO-1976/79 + O45-1987/90, O50-1993/95

Ross Norman (NZL), WO-1986 + O40-1999

▲ David, above, won the World Open title eight times; a record, although Nour El Sherbini is currently standing at seven.

Massaro makes it

2014 was quite a year for Laura Massaro. She had been runner-up in the World championship two years earlier, then went to Penang, the home of Nicol David, the holder, and came away with the title. David was beaten by Nour El Sherbini in the semis and Massaro beat the Egyptian 11-9 in their deciding final game. She followed this by leading England to the World Team title later in the same year.

Her strengths – fitness, volleying and stubbornness – had already taken her to the British Open crown in 2013, becoming the first English woman's winner after Lisa Opie in 1991; Three years later she lost another World Open final, but she followed it in 2017 by winning a second British Open title. Massaro showed her durability and consistency by staying in the world top ten for eleven unbroken years, including four months at number one.

▲ Husband Danny enjoys the moment after Massaro won the British Open 2013.

First from France

Camille Serme (right) may not have won a World championship, and only narrowly missed out on world number one spot, reaching two; but she is in the record books as the first French woman to win majors. From the Paris suburb of Créteil, she won the British Open in 2015, the US Open a year later and the Tournament of Champions in 2017 and 2020, as well as the World Games title in 2017. Her success was due to good movement and high-quality driving, with the addition of French finesse to ensure opponents were unsettled.

Unbroken spans

The women's and men's record holders for longest unbroken months in the world top 10 are Nicol David's 177 (Jan 2004 – Sept 2018), and Mohamed ElShorbagy who up to June 2024 has been in the top 10 since December 2010, so 162 months so far.

◀ SQUASHTV presenters
Joey Barrington (left)
and Vanessa Atkinson.

Broadcast game changer

The launch of
SQUASHTV
in 2010 was a
game-changer
for the sport.
Before then local

broadcasters filmed the later rounds of major
events for national broadcast. The tapes were
taken back to the tours to produce highlights
programmes from the footage for international
broadcasters; the quality being variable,
without uniformity of style; and, importantly, no
live option for international audiences.

PSA, led by Chairman Ziad Al-Turki and CEO
Alex Gough, invested in a production set-
up, brought event rights back in-house, sent
a team to film, provided enhanced quality,
ensured uniform presentation and delivered
live-output options online and to broadcasters.
It meant that an online channel dedicated
exclusively to squash was now available,
enabling all show-court rounds to be viewed.

SQUASHTV has also provided broadcast
opportunities beyond just a widening range of
PSA events, enhancements have continued
in camera quality, slow-motion, graphics and
video referee review to take squash further into
the broadcast mainstream.

Ziad's key role

**Ziad Al-Turki, was elected
chairman of PSA in 2008, and in
addition to leading the creation of
SQUASHTV and overseeing the merger
of the men's and women's tours, he has also played a
crucial role in the running of the PSA World Tour Finals. In
2010 Ziad had brought the men's World championship to
his nation, Saudi Arabia, and in 2018 he played a key role in
staging the first ever professional women's squash event in
the kingdom.**

Side entry!

The ASB court company recognised that by removing the door they
could reducing the number of back-wall joints to improve the clarity
of the broadcast for the main camera. So, in 2012 they produced a
showcourt with doors in each side wall leaving the back wall with fewer
panels and no hinges. Players would enter and exit from their own side.

▶ Nick Matthew uses a side exit.

Squash in stations

Another innovative location was a waiting room in New York's Grand Central Terminal, the front wall being passed by tens of thousands of commuters every day. It became the home of the Tournament of Champions in 1995. This was preceded in the late 1980s in England when Bristol Temple Meads Station in England saw a court built on the track-bed of the original 1840s terminus, with seating on the platforms.

1. The Grand Central Terminal waiting room, New York.
2. Between the platforms at Temple Meads, Bristol.
3. Chicago's Union Station.

Most recently Chicago's Union Station has been used as a venue too - for the World championships in 2019 and 2023.

Squash 'n light show

The 2011 men's World Team championship in Paderborn, Germany, showed how promoters could innovatively embrace the possibilities of enhancing the on-site and broadcast presentation of events. In this case the LightPower visual company rigged a light show that flooded the show court between matches.

The late developer

Englishman Nick Matthew once said, '*You do not have to be the best when you are 12, 13 or even aged 25. It is part of the journey, doing the right things, being motivated and setting yourself apart. That can happen later and people develop at different times'.* As a player who achieved his greatest success in his thirties, his squash prime was unusually late. He was already supremely fit and very determined, but to achieve the success he did, re-modelling his game was needed. His swing was changed, the ball now taken even earlier, straight volleying to the fore. These adaptations were made during a time-period in which he also experienced significant shoulder and knee injuries which required time out from the tour and could have snuffed out his career.

While the first of his three British Open titles was won in 2006, the other two in 2009/12 were during his purple patch. Aged thirty he took his first World championship in 2010, retained it in 2011 and won a third in 2013. Those titles, along with a further spell at world number one at the start of 2014 when aged 33 were a great achievement, but he was not done yet. Later in 2014 he retained the Commonwealth Games individual gold that he had won in 2010.

Nick Matthew reaches for the ball against Amr Shabana at the US Open 2012.

▶ Matthew celebrates beating Ali Farag in the quarter finals of the US Open 2016.

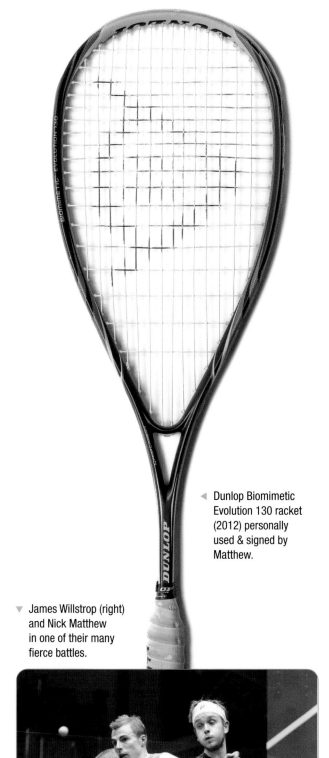

◀ Dunlop Biomimetic
Evolution 130 racket
(2012) personally
used & signed by
Matthew.

▼ James Willstrop (right)
and Nick Matthew
in one of their many
fierce battles.

Battling with Nick

Born three years later than his English teammate, James
Willstrop became world number one for eleven months in
2012, and followed Matthew in becoming Commonwealth
Games individual champion in 2018 aged 34; but he narrowly
missed out on several major titles. With a mobility belying
his height, he was runner-up in three British Open finals,
including 2008 when he lost 13-11 in the deciding game to
David Palmer; and he reached the World championship final
losing to his great rival Matthew in 2010.

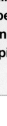

Gaultier (left) winning his 2015 World Championship final against Egyptian Omar Mosaad.

Masterful masters

When the British Open was staged in London in 1976 it incorporated the inaugural men's World Open championship. Additionally, the ISRF accorded similar status to Veterans and Vintage events (the colloquial titles for the Over 45 and Over 55 age groups). Following this debut age group events became appended to various world team and individual championships until 1991. In that year New Zealand hosted the first World Masters championships, which were staged purely for mature age players, as they have been biennially since in five-year bands from Over 35 through to Over 80.

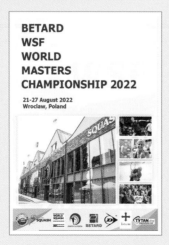

BETARD
WSF
WORLD
MASTERS
CHAMPIONSHIP 2022

21-27 August 2022
Wroclaw, Poland

The other veteran champion

Gregory Gaultier, like Matthew, experienced great success in the later years of his 22-year tour career; his earliest playing period saw him missing out due to being volcanic, distracted and generally stressed on court. Calming down brought rewards.

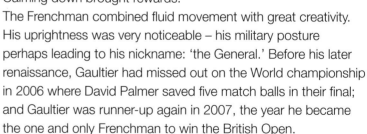

The Frenchman combined fluid movement with great creativity. His uprightness was very noticeable – his military posture perhaps leading to his nickname: 'the General.' Before his later renaissance, Gaultier had missed out on the World championship in 2006 where David Palmer saved five match balls in their final; and Gaultier was runner-up again in 2007, the year he became the one and only Frenchman to win the British Open.

Fast forward to his calmer phase, after he was runner-up in the Worlds twice more (2011/13), he became world champion in 2015, one month short of his 33rd birthday, as well as winning two more British Opens (2014/17). In January 2018, he became the first player to play 700 tour matches and he continued playing even after a serious knee injury that year. He eventually retired at the age of 38 in 2021.

THE WOMEN WHO HAVE REACHED THE PINNACLE –
SQUASH'S WORLD JUNIOR CHAMPIONS

1981
LISA OPIE
England

1983
ROBYN FRIDAY
Australia

1985
LUCY SOUTTER
England

1987
SARAH FITZ-GERALD
Australia

1989
DONNA VARDY
England

1991
CASSIE JACKMAN
England

1993
RACHAEL GRINHAM
Australia

1995
JADE WILSON
New Zealand

1997
TANIA BAILEY
England

1999.2001
NICOL DAVID
Malaysia

2003
OMNEYA ABDEL KAWY
Egypt

2005.2007
RANEEM EL WELILY
Egypt

2009.2012.2013
NOUR EL SHERBINI
Egypt

2010
AMANDA SOBHY
USA

2011
NOUR EL TAYEB
Egypt

2014
HABIBA MOHAMED
Egypt

2015.2016
NOURAN GOHAR
Egypt

2017.2018
ROWAN ELARABY
Egypt

2019
HANIA EL HAMMAMY
Egypt

2022.2023.2024
AMINA ORFI
Egypt

www.squashlibrary.info
info@squashlibrary.info

Squash archive and information resource

Squash Info

WORLD SQUASH LIBRARY
THE SQUASH RESULTS & ARCHIVE HUBS

Most photos kindly provided by Steve Line

Squash and the Olympics

Almost from the birth of multi-sided viewing showcourts in the early 1980s, squash began pushing for a place on the programme of the Olympic Games. The first brochure was produced for the 1992 Barcelona edition, but a lack of effort combined with the less-than-ideal quality of squash broadcasting contributed to the attempts failing.

However, at the IOC session in 2005 squash unexpectedly came very close to securing a place for London 2012 when baseball and softball were surprisingly taken out. Squash was voted top of the list of bidding sports but was below the majority needed for a sport to be added and missed out.

Four years later, in 2009, the sports for Rio 2016 were decided. Squash was beaten by the more media rights-strong golf and rugby sevens.

'I would happily trade all my seven world titles for Olympic Gold' NICOL DAVID

SQUASH AND THE 2020 OLYMPIC GAMES

▲ After giving this memorable quote she won an eighth world title.

Squash, the Olympic sport

SQUASH was admitted to the Olympic movement in December 1985, an important development for the sport and one which will aid its worldwide growth.

The recognition will make it possible for many ISRF member nations to get financial aid from their governments and it is also hoped that it will stimulate interest in the sport from countries that either have no recognised national association or do not yet play the game.

RIGHT: How squash was formally admitted to the Olympic Movement

▲ The first brochure for 1992.

Squash-an Olympic sport in Barcelona?

THE International Squash Rackets Federation and the Spanish Federation of Squash (FES) share the common goal of seeking squash's acceptance as a demonstration sport in Barcelona in 1992.

The case for squash, as stated by the ISRF, has been presented elsewhere and the FES would strongly argue that the development of the sport in Spain adds a lot of weight to the claim to be represented in Barcelona.

1. In the period from 1978 to 1987 the sport has grown from being virtually unknown to a level of 100,000 players and the projected number of players by 1992 is expected to approach one million.
2. In Barcelona there are already in existence a number of squash clubs capable of staging world class events, with further clubs expected to be completed by 1992.
3. Catalan is the region in Spain having the most clubs and Barcelona therefore is a logical centre for the staging of an Olympic squash event.
4. Spain has already organised events of world class and has experienced officials ready to co-operate with the Olympic Organising Committee.
5. Squash in Spain has reached its present level of development without State aid and is therefore shown to be an aggressive and capable sport.
6. The King of Spain is interested in squash and has twice received the officials of the FES.
7. The FES is well regarded by the International and European Squash Federations for its progress and development of squash.

OLYMPIC EVENT IN BARCELONA

THE ISRF envisage that an Olympic squash event in Barcelona would involve no more than 16 national teams selected from all the major squash playing regions of the world.

Such an event would be played over a five day period and would be self financing.

It is anticipated that the initial rounds would be played at the leading clubs in Barcelona and culminate in a grand final using a portable transparent court.

OLYMPIC SQUASH PLEDGE
AN OLYMPIC GOLD MEDAL WOULD BE THE ULTIMATE PRIZE IN SQUASH!

▲ WSF President Jahangir Khan gives a player participation pledge to IOC President Jacques Rogge in 2008.

▲ Tennis star Roger Federer supported the 2020 bid.

Perseverance pays off

Then for the next Games in 2020, the IOC committed to taking out a sport to make way for a new one. Wrestling was removed, only to be replaced by the 'new' sport of ... wrestling!

For the Tokyo 2020 games the IOC introduced host picks for the first time. The Japanese requested baseball and karate – both hugely popular there, with the IOC's choice of surfing, skateboarding and wall climbing added too. This desire to include youth-orientated activities to enhance the urban credentials of the IOC was clear, with breakdancing added for Paris 2024.

These decisions led to disenchantment with the process amongst the squash community and calls for WSF & PSA to stop wasting time and resources on the fruitless task. However, for the 2028 Games in Los Angeles the sport had some leverage via American sports and media leadership; and this paid off so that squash will be dining at the top table of sport for the first time after forty years of trying.

▲ The WSF / PSA bid team for 2024.

SQUASH
LA28 OLYMPIC GAMES

Mohamed ElShorbagy has Simon Rösner (GER) under pressure.

▲ Mohamed ElShorbagy and Matthew battle.

From Alexandria to Somerset

15-year-old Mohamed ElShorbagy left the Egyptian city of Alexandria in 2006 to nestle under the wing of squash coach Jonah Barrington at Millfield School in Somerset, England. A year later younger brother Marwan joined him. The brothers each went on to win the World Junior title twice, Mohamed in 2008/09, Marwan following in 2011/12; and while both have gone on to senior success, Marwan reaching third spot in the world, Mohamed has reached still greater heights.

Powerful, imposing and durable, his fifty months atop the world rankings in the seven years from November 2014 attest to Mohamed's consistency. He reached five World championship finals (2012/14/17/21/22), only winning the title in 2017 in Manchester, England, where the runner-up was Marwan his brother. Marwan, lighter and more subtle in style, lost in five games in his only world final experience. Mohamed, engaging but forthright, had not seen eye-to-eye with the Egyptian Squash Federation for some time, so used his residential qualification to change allegiance to England in 2022, followed a year later by his brother.

El Welily and Momen

Raneem El Welily has undoubtedly been one of the most athletic and extravagantly talented players to grace a court, but sometimes beset by error-prone spells in a match. A two-time World Junior champion (2005/07), she had already lost two prior World championship finals, when in December 2017, aged 28, she scored her ultimate victory. By then, her exciting squash had become steadier, her coaches

▲ El Welily celebrating her World championship with husband Momen.

had dampened down the stress levels, and support from her 2014 marriage to fellow top-liner Tarek Momen helped too. El Welily was World championship runner-up for the third time in 2019; before becoming only one of a tiny handful of players who retired as world number one. She did so in 2020, having spent a career total of 23 months in the top spot.

Husband Tarek Momen had his career pinnacle at age 31 when he won the World championship in November 2019, having been runner-up in the previous one. Similar to Raneem in terms of being fast but inconsistent, they inspired and balanced each other. A husband and wife, both world champions, a first for squash!

Raneem El Welily.

Momen playing Paul Coll.

The effortless Egyptian

Karim Abdel Gawad seems to cruise languidly around the court, but the talented stroke-maker has coupled his gifted play with pace to take him to titles. He won the World Championship in 2016, became world number one, albeit for one month only in May 2017; and was a member of the Egyptian team that won the World Team title in 2017 and 2019. It is only a series of injuries including plantar fasciitis that have prevented him from scoring more major success.

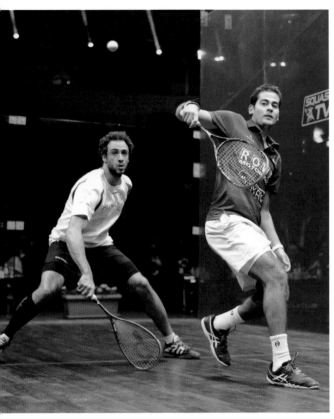

▲ Karim Abdel Gawad winning his 2016 World Open final against Ashour, who had to retire in the fourth game.

▲ Covid (2020-22) meant play was suspended for long periods and squash clubs forced to close.

WORLD CHAMPIONSHIP PRIZE FUNDS							
MEN'S				WOMEN'S			
YEAR	VENUE	FUND		YEAR	VENUE	FUND	
1976	London, England		a	1976	Brisbane, Australia	$4,500	
1977	Adelaide, Australia	$40,000		1977			
1978				1978			
1979	Toronto, Canada	$50,000		1979	Sheffield, England	$4,750	
1980	Adelaide, Australia	$50,000		1980			
1981	Toronto, Canada	$50,000		1981	Toronto, Canada	$12,500	
1982	Birmingham, England	$48,000		1982			
1983	Munich, Germany	$30,000		1983	Perth, Australia	$18,000	
1984	Karachi, Pakistan	$30,000		1984			
1985	Cairo, Egypt	$50,000		1985	Dublin, Ireland	$22,200	
1986	Toulouse, France	$55,000		1986			
1987	Birmingham, England	$101,000		1987	Auckland, New Zealand	$30,000	
1988	Amsterdam, Netherlands	$82,000		1988			
1989	Kuala Lumpur, Malaysia	$85,000		1989	Warmond, Netherlands	$40,000	
1990	Toulouse, France	$110,000		1990	Sydney, Australia	$29,000	
1991	Adelaide, Australia	$130,000		1991			
1992	Johannesburg, South Africa	$160,000		1992	Vancouver, Canada	$35,000	
1993	Karachi, Pakistan	$120,000		1993	Johannesburg, S Africa	$45,000	
1994	Barcelona, Spain	$150,000		1994	St Peter Port, Guernsey	$64,000	
1995	Nicosia, Cyprus	$110,000		1995	Hong Kong	$58,000	
1996	Karachi, Pakistan	$130,000		1996	Petaling Jaya, Malaysia	$65,000	
1997	Petaling Jaya, Malaysia	$130,000		1997	Sydney, Australia	$75,000	
1998	Doha, Qatar	$175,000		1998	Stuttgart, Germany	$70,000	
1999	Cairo, Egypt	$170,000		1999	Seattle, USA	$80,000	
2000			c	2000	Edinburgh, Scotland	$80,000	
2001			c	2001	Melbourne, Australia	$69,500	
2002	Antwerp, Belgium	$155,000		2002	Doha, Qatar	$102,500	
2003	Lahore, Pakistan	$170,000		2003	Hong Kong, China	$57,500	
2004	Doha, Qatar	$120,000		2004	Kuala Lumpur, Mas	$75,000	
2005	Hong Kong, China	$170,000		2005	Hong Kong, China	$72,500	
2006	Cairo, Egypt	$152,500		2006	Belfast, N Ireland	$112,500	
2007	Hamilton, Bermuda	$175,000		2007	Madrid, Spain	$114,000	
2008	Manchester, England	$215,000		2008	Manchester, England	$114,000	
2009	Green Island Resort, Kuwait	$277,500		2009	Amsterdam, Netherlands	$118,000	
2010	Al-Khobar, Saudi Arabia	$327,500		2010	Sharm El Sheikh, Egypt	$147,000	
2011	Rotterdam, Ned	$275,000		2011	Rotterdam, Netherlands	$143,000	
2012	Doha, Qatar	$325,000		2012	Cayman Islands	$188,000	
2013	Manchester, England	$325,000		2014	Cairo, Egypt	$135,000	
2014	Doha, Qatar	$325,000		2014	Penang, Malaysia	$150,000	
2015	Bellevue, Washington, USA	$325,000		2016	Kuala Lumpur, Mas	$185,000	b
2016	Cairo, Egypt	$325,000		2017	El Gouna, Egypt	$279,000	b
2017	Manchester, England	$325,000		2017	Manchester, England	$165,000	b
2019	Doha, Qatar	$335,000	b	2019	Cairo, Egypt	$430,000	b
2019	Chicago, USA	$500,000	b	2019	Chicago, USA	$500,000	b
2021	Chicago, USA	$500,000		2021	Chicago, USA	$500,000	
2022	Cairo, Egypt	$550,000		2022	Cairo, Egypt	$550,000	
2023	Chicago, USA	$525,500		2023	Chicago, USA	$525,500	
2024	Cairo, Egypt	$575,000		2024	Cairo, Egypt	$575,00	

Jointly staged 2005/08/11/17 and 2019 onwards

Prize funds include added sums for benefits e,g. hotel, for men, and from 1985 women

Women's held biennially initially

a Additional title for British Open winner

b Events delayed / played twice in a year

c Not played (including 2020, Covid)

Touchpad squash

Court front walls have been plaster, panel and even glass, but by 2016 they could be turned into a touchpad when *interactiveSQUASH* was born. Developed by German entrepreneur Markos Kern, squash joined the digital age; touching the wall to access a variety of games and training routines. Sensors tracking the ball, graphics projected onto the front wall; and with other applications available too, it signposted new possibilities for future generations.

Appealing times

Once TV production started to be managed in-house by the tours it became possible to instantly playback rallies so that decisions could be reviewed. From 2011 at filmed events, if players have disputed the decision of a referee, they could now appeal to the video referee, who would have alternative angles and slow-motion options available – which they and spectators can view too on screens, adding another layer of interest.

Public park courts

Historically there were some outdoor courts dotted around in hot places; with concrete floors designed to destroy knee and ankle joints! However, in 2018 in a bid to develop the outdoor market, a public court developed by ASB was erected at Hamilton Fish Park in New York City for summer play. The floor featured weather-resistant boards installed on top of an elastic sub-structure that would allow rainwater to drain away.

Plenty in Philly, Huge at Hasta

The world's largest squash facility, the Hasta La Vista club, opened in Wroclaw, Poland, in 2012. It increased to no less than 33 courts, including a showcourt that could be built in the club's ten-court badminton hall. The centre, not surprisingly, has hosted larger events such as the World and European Masters.

As courts in the USA transitioned to softball, Philadelphia regained its primary squash city status. By November 2022 one road - 33rd Street - was such a focus for squash that the city re-named it 'Squash Way'.

On it were Drexel University's Kline & Specter Squash Center and the Penn Squash Center; but when the US Squash dream of a national facility became a reality in 2021 there were no less than 37 courts within a couple of blocks. The Arlen Specter US Squash Center, contributed eighteen courts to the total.

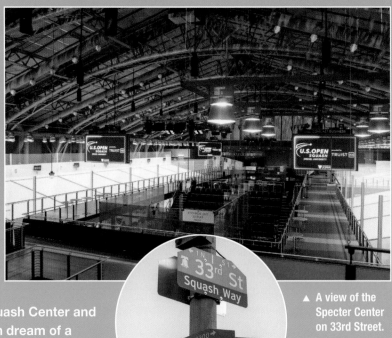

▲ A view of the Specter Center on 33rd Street.

Squash showcased at Youth Olympics

The IOC invited squash to be a showcase sport for the Buenos Aires 2018 Summer Youth Olympic Games. Skateboarding and sport climbing moved up from the 2014 Youth Games to the 2020 Olympics; but there was no such stepping stone for squash to the Paris 2024 Olympic Games as had been hoped, even though it marked the first Olympic inclusion for squash.

Shawn DeLierre.

El Hammamy diving against Gohar.

Winning length

In January 2015 Canadian Shawn DeLierre, expanded his listing of long matches by managing a record-breaking 170-minute epic before finally losing to Leo Au from Hong Kong at the Holtrand Gas City Pro-Am in Canada. The match ended with a 78-minute final game, eclipsing the now second longest match, 166 minutes (for only four games!) in which Jahangir Khan beat Gamal Awad in 1983. To date, DeLierre has played in three of the four longest ever squash matches. The women's record so far is the heroic 130 minutes that it took Nouran Gohar to beat Hania El Hammamy in the final of the 2023 PSA World Tour Finals.

England's strangleholds broken

England were unbeaten going into the 8th men's European Team championship in 1980. For Sweden it was third time lucky when they finally became the second nation to take the title, after losing in the previous two finals. Sweden won again in 1983, but it wasn't until 2015 that France became the second mainland European men's winners (pic). They won again in 2017/18.

Meanwhile, England's Women were unbeaten for the first 32 editions right through to 2010 when the Netherlands (pictured) took the title.

▲ The winning 2010 Dutch team. Left to right: Nicole Beumer (coach), Orla Noom, Margriet Huisman, Annelize Naude, Vanessa Atkinson.

Women and men united

On 1 January 2015 squash, unlike many sports including tennis and golf, became amalgamated at tour level when the women's (WISPA, then briefly WSA) and men's (PSA) tours joined together under the PSA banner.

▲ The French 2015 winning squad.

El Sherbini, a record breaker

Nour El Sherbini was a squash prodigy. Physically strong for a 13-year-old, with abounding talent and no fear, in 2009 she became the youngest ever winner of the World Junior (under 19) title. Indeed, El Sherbini (born 1995) broke other records for the World Junior event, winning the title three times from four final appearances (2009/12/13, r-up in 2011).

The girl from Alexandria also started winning senior tour events aged 14, and in April 2016 she won the World championship for the first time aged 20. This meant more records – the first Egyptian women's winner and the youngest to do so. Since then she has amassed seven world crowns (2016/17/19[twice]/21/22/23) leaving her needing one more to equal Nicol David's record eight, an attempt that failed in 2024 when beaten by Nouran Gohar in the final.

Celebrating her 7th world title in 2023.

Able to dominate so many opponents with her attacking verve and so many shots in her armoury, she would also point to a serenity on court that has helped her greatly. *'Staying calm has helped me a lot in life'*, she has said. Off court she has needed to remain composed in the face of knee issues that have required surgery. Impressively, her second world title was won having not played an event for four months while sidelined by the problem.

El Sherbini, whose nickname is 'the Warrior Princess', on the cover of the 2019 World championship programme.

After taking top spot in the rankings in May 2016, El Sherbini has been ahead of the pack for most of the time since. And with four World Team titles (2012/16/18/22) already in the bag, there may be more of everything to come from the outstanding player of her generation.

El Sherbini drops against Nouran Gohar at the Tournament of Champions 2024.

Gohar finally triumphs

Since fellow Egyptian Nouran Gohar became world number one for the first time in July 2020, she and El Sherbini traded top spot but not World championships, as that title had been firmly in the grip of El Sherbini…. until 2024. Gohar did have three US Opens (2019/21/22) to her name though, along with the 2019 British Open. But in 2024 after losing in three world finals she finally beat El Sherbini to take the world title and beat her again a few weeks later to win her second British Open crown.

Renowned for her ferocious hitting, Gohar's game was described by Raneem El Welily thus, *'When Nouran is in her rhythm and hitting the ball hard and clean it is really difficult to break her game down. She is super strong physically, with a tremendous will to win.'* While she has a construction engineering career to fall back on, her ferocity, and a particularly strong backhand have taken her forward to become an enduring top-liner.

Age matters

The youngest world champions have been:
Nour El Sherbini (EGY): 20y 5m (in April 2016)
Jahangir Khan (PAK): 17y 11m (in Nov 1981)
The oldest world champions have been:
Heather McKay (AUS): 37y 7m (in March 1979)
Geoff Hunt (AUS): 33y 6m (in Oct 1980)

Gohar on the move against Amanda Sobhy (USA, left).

Jahangir Khan (left) and Susan Devoy (right) were the first two 'legends' admitted to the new PSA Hall of Fame at the British Open 2024, shown here together with winners Asal and Gohar.

China hosts

A World championship landed in mainland China for the first time in 2018 when the women's World Team event was played at the Xi-Gang Stadium (right) in the city of Dalian. The stadium featured four permanent showcourts to which two more showcourts were built in the gymnasium for the event. In another landmark, it became the first time that the world team event was played entirely on showcourts.

Number of facilities worldwide
13.000

Number of courts worldwide
40.000

Facilities over Continents

- 14% Africa
- 21% Asia
- 33% Europe
- 6% Oceania
- 13% North America
- 13% South America

Where the courts are

A 2024 survey by Squash Facilities network estimated that there are around 13,000 facilities with 40,000 courts around the world, with one third in Europe and Asia having the second largest share with 21%. The decreasing number of courts in some 'mature' squash nations such as UK and Australia, contrasts greatly with continents like Asia. Much of that area, especially China, is featuring a growth spurt at the present time.

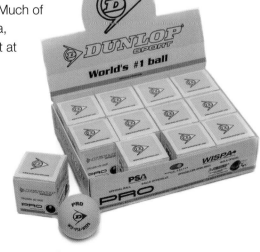

Satomi Watanabe provided more evidence of the international spread of elite success when the Japanese player won the Optasia championship women's event in London in March 2024.

Box of 12 white yellow double dot Dunlop balls (c2010), for use on glass courts.

Farag in full flow.

Four times Farag

Ali Farag is a four-time world champion (2019/21/22/23) who clearly has a soft spot for the USA. He studied at Harvard University (gaining a degree in mechanical engineering) and has also won three of his current four World championship titles in Chicago, together with 2022 in his home city of Cairo.

Coming from an academic family, Farag (born 1992) was torn between which professional career to progress. The light-weight Egyptian chose squash and was initially influenced by coach Mike Way at Harvard. *'He reads his opponents and feels the right shot selection'*, Way has said. Long striding, efficient movement coupled with the ability to manoeuvre opponents while looking for an opening have been his modus operandi. Top spot in the rankings was first gained in March 2019, and while it was not unbroken, he was still holding the position going into 2024.

Farag at the front against Max Lee (HKG).

More US connections

In 2016 Farag married Nour El Tayeb, also born in Cairo and with similar Stateside connections. In 2011 she won the World Junior title at Harvard, where Farag studied, having lost in the previous two finals. Later, in 2017, the pair scored a unique double triumph on the same day, both winning their US Open finals. El Tayeb had reached the world top three in 2018, got to the final of the 2019 World championship where Nour El Sherbini thwarted her, and after the birth of their daughter in July 2021 she managed a return to the top five.

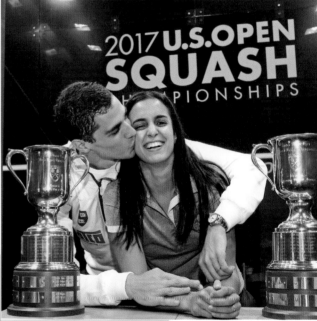
▲ Ali & Nour, US Open champions 2017.

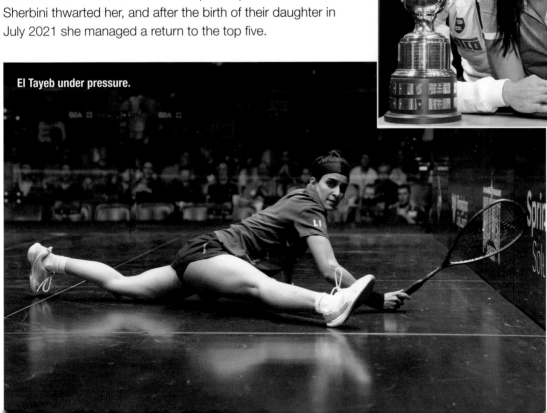
El Tayeb under pressure.

225

The first Kiwi

When Paul Coll (left) won the British Open in 2021 he became the first New Zealander to take the men's title. He followed it up in March 2022 by also becoming the first male Kiwi to take World number one spot – in a year that saw him retain his British Open crown and also take gold at the Commonwealth Games. Nicknamed 'Superman' for his super-strength and resilience, his happiness to patiently endure punishing rallies has made him difficult to dislodge in matches.

Asal atop

Aged just 21, Mostafa Asal (right) ascended to number one in the world rankings in January 2023, a spot he held for three months. However, his rise was not smooth. He had won the World Junior title twice (2018/19), and had a hat-trick of World Tour Final titles (2021/22/23); but his blossoming career has not been without disciplinary issues. He bounced back strongly in 2024 and reached the World championship final before being beaten by Diego Elias. An aggressive and forceful player, gifted too, his victory over Ali Farag in the final of the 2024 British Open meant another of his extravagant celebratory routines was seen in Birmingham.

◀ Elias executes, Asal appeals.

Playing at full length!

Colombian Miguel Angel Rodriguez (above) would wow the crowds with his diving, bouncing back up and continuing the rally, but that has not been his only claim to fame. Stocky, and all-action, Rodriguez became the highest ranked South American before the emergence of Peru's Diego Elias, reaching number four in the world during 2015. Then in 2018, aged 32, he won the British Open, beating Mohamed ElShorbagy in the final – the only South American holder so far.

Squash's archive

The World Squash Library was founded in Southgate, London, UK in October 2019 by Andrew Shelley, intending that the sport would have an archive of books, handbooks, publications, documents, photos, films etc that would be freely available and preserved for future generations.

WORLD SQUASH LIBRARY

Elias takes over

Diego Elias was a double winner of the World Junior title in 2014/15. Also in 2015 he reached the final of the PanAm Games where Rodriguez beat him – and though the next two finals in 2019/23 may have featured the same players, the outcome was reversed, with Elias, from Lima, Peru, winning both. Once likened by Geoff Hunt to Jansher Khan, early mentoring from Jonathon Power and coaching by his father Jose Manuel, the Peruvian national coach, Elias's rise has been steady and inexorable. Already a multi-major event winner, for the months of April and May 2023 he became the first South American to sit on top of the world rankings. A year later in May 2024 his rise was cemented when he beat Mostafa Asal in Cairo to become the first world squash champion from South America.

▶ Elias happily poses as world champion 2024.

227

SQUASH HISTORY TIMELINE

Key dates for the international game, with fuller details on many in the decade chapters.

1800s

Squash in its original version first played in courtyards at Harrow School, near London, England.

1865

1st squash courts are opened at Harrow School.

1883

A squash court is built at a home in Oxford, England.

1884

1st squash courts in USA are built at St. Paul's School in Concord, New Hampshire.

1894

1st magazine article on squash is published in Boys Own Paper.

1901

1st book on squash, 'The Game of Squash' by Eustace Miles, is published.

1902

1st court at a club in Ireland is built at the Fitzwilliam LTC in Dublin.

1903

1st inter-club squash league worldwide is founded in Philadelphia.

1904

1st court at a club in Canada is built at the St. John's Tennis Club in Newfoundland.

London's leading club, Bath Club, adds squash courts.

The US squash federation, the world's oldest national governing body, is founded.

1906

1st court at a club in South Africa is built at the Country Club, Johannesburg.

1907

1st court in New Zealand is built at the Christchurch Club.

1st US Nationals are held in Philadelphia.

1908

Tennis & Rackets Association (T&RA) in London forms a squash sub-committee.

1910

South Africa forms a national federation & hosts its 1st Amateur championship.

1912

RMS Titanic sails from England with a squash court before sinking.

1913

1st court at a club in Australia is built at the Melbourne Club.

1915

Canadian national federation is formed.

1920

US squash federation standardises its 'narrow' courts.

1st Professional Championship of the British Isles is won by Charles Read.

1922

1st women's British Open is held at Queen's Club in London.

Bath Club Cup, a London squash league, is started.

1st international match, the annual Lapham Cup contest (USA v Canada).

1923

English squash clubs form a sub-committee under the T&RA.

It decides the standard size of a court and sets the tin height.

1st British Amateur championship.

1924

1st overseas travelling team, Great Britain touring side to North America.

1926

1st Drysdale Cup (now the British Junior Open boys U19).

T&RA issues official rules for squash.

HiHo scoring switches from 15-point to 9-point scoring.

1927

In France 4 courts are opened in Paris at the Société Sportive du Jeu de Paume.

1928

T&RA's squash committee in London separates to form the Squash Rackets Association.

1st US Women's championship is held.

1st Australian championship.

1930

1st men's British Open.

1931

Egypt forms a national federation.

1932

1st New Zealand Nationals.

F.D. Amr Bey wins the 1st of 5 men's British Open titles.

1st magazine featuring squash, 'Squash Rackets, Fives, Tennis and Rackets' is published in UK.

1933

1st International women's match played for the Wolfe-Noel Cup (USA v GB).

1934

Thames House in London with 15 courts becomes the world's largest club at that point.

Margot Lumb wins the 1st of 5 women's British Open titles.

Women's Squash Rackets Association (UK) is formed.

1935

Lansdowne Club in London opens, featuring the Bruce Court with a capacity for 200 spectators.

1948

Men's British Open ceases to be a two-person challenge and becomes a knock-out tournament.

1st national federation to have a full-time employee and an office is British SRA.

1950

Janet Morgan wins the 1st of 10 women's British Open titles.

1951

Hashim Khan wins the 1st of 7 men's British Open titles.

1953

India forms a national federation.

1954

1st United States Open.

1956

Racket shafts (not heads) may be made of other materials, not just wood.

1958

Biggest court viewing gallery of the time is built at Cairo University - capacity 500.

1959

1st time a squash match is televised in a local broadcast at US Open in Pittsburgh.

1961

1st overseas winner of British Junior Open, Peter Gerlow from Denmark.

1962

Heather McKay wins the 1st of 16 women's British Open titles.

1964

1st England v Australia women's Test match is held.

1965

A small glass window is added to a court door in Hobart, Australia, to enable filming.

1966

Birkenhead Squash Rackets Club in England unveils a court with a partial glass back wall.

Jonah Barrington wins the 1st of 6 men's British Open titles.

1967

1st meeting of the world federation (ISRF).

1st men's World Team championship (with accompanying individual amateur event).

1968

1st entirely transparent back wall court is built at the University of Pennsylvania in Philadelphia.

1969

Geoff Hunt wins the 1st of 8 men's British Open titles.

1970

Ball speeds begin to be indicated by coloured dots.

1971

1st all-glass suspended assembly back wall is built at Abbeydale Park in Sheffield, England.

1st edition of Squash Player Magazine (UK).

1973

1st regional federation is formed - Europe.

1st European Team championship.

1974

Men's International Squash Players Association (ISPA) is founded.

Women's British Open allows professionals to enter.

Wembley Squash Centre opens in London, England.

1976

1st World Open championships are played (the men's is combined with the British Open).

1st World Masters.

Racketball (now Squash57) is introduced.

PIA Squash Complex opens in Karachi, Pakistan.

1977

1st men's rankings are published (seeding lists prior).

1978

1st tournament on a portable court with a glass back wall in Stockholm, Sweden.

1979

1st women's World Team championship.

1st time squash is included in the Pacific (Oceania) Games.

1980

1st men's World Junior Team and Individual championships are held.

Squash goes 'open' as amateur status ends.

1st British Open played on a portable court, at the Wembley Conference Centre.

Asian Squash Federation is formed.

1981

World Open played on a portable court with a glass front and back wall in Toronto, Canada.

Jahangir Khan wins the 1st of 6 men's World titles.

1st women's World Junior Individual championship.

1st Asian Team & Individual championships.

1982

1st men's and women's British Open held together.

Jahangir Khan wins the 1st of 10 men's British Open titles.

1st four-sided showcourt is at the World Masters (male pros) in Leicester, England.

Rackets made entirely of materials other than wood permitted.

1983

Coloured clothing restrictions are discontinued.

1st coloured floor (blue) and white ball used at the French Open.

1984

Susan Devoy wins the 1st of 8 women's British Open titles.

British Racketball Association formed.

1st AGM of the Women's International Squash Players Association.

1985

1st Women's Junior Team championship.

US Open switches from hardball to international softball.

1986

IOC grants official recognition to squash.

1987

3,526 attendance at the men's World Team finals at Royal Albert Hall in London, England.

Jansher Khan wins the 1st of 8 men's World titles.

1989

Second serve rule dropped.

Men's pro squash switches to 15-point, point-per-rally scoring & begins using 17 inch / 43 cm tin.

PSA men's tour reaches $1m prize money.

Pan American Squash Federation formed.

1990

1st World championship to have more than one showcourt (Men's Open, Toulouse).

1991

1st stand-alone World Masters.

Rackets with larger strung surfaces (up to 500cm2) permitted.

1992

The International Squash Rackets Federation becomes World Squash Federation.

The Oceania & African regional Federations formed.

The dimensions of doubles courts are standardised.

1993

PSA formed by the merging of the men's pro association (ISPA) with the hardball pro association.

1995

1st time squash in the Pan American Games.

1st time Tournament of Champions is staged in Grand Central Terminal in New York.

1996

1st World Cup.

1st event played in front of the Great Pyramids of Giza, Egypt.

1st urban youth programme, SquashBusters in Boston, USA.

1997

1st World Doubles.

1st time squash in World Games.

1998

1st time squash in the Commonwealth Games.

1st time squash in the Asian Games.

Men's rankings go from 2 months to monthly.

1999

Protective eyewear mandated for under 19 age players.

Double yellow dot balls produced.

2001

Women's rankings go from bimonthly to monthly.

2002

1st World Squash Day.

2003

1st time squash is included in the African Games.

2004

Men's tour moves from PAR15 to PAR11.

1st internet live stream at the Tournament of Champions.

Squashinfo.com starts.

2005

Nicol David wins the 1st of 8 women's World titles.

1st time M/W World championships played together.

2007

Two sisters, Rachael & Natalie Grinham, play the World Open final.

2008

A widened court width for international doubles is set.

The women's pro tour switches to 11-point, point-per-rally scoring.

2009

Nour El Sherbini becomes the youngest women's Junior World champion, aged 13.

2010

SQUASHTV launched.

2011

1st use of a video referee and player appeal system.

2012

WSF publishes standard Racketball rules, including ball specifications.

Hasta La Vista Club in Wroclaw, Poland opens, enlarging into the world's largest club with 33 courts.

The tin height for international doubles events is dropped to 13 inch / 33 cm.

2015

PSA and WSA (formerly WISPA) merge to create a new PSA.

Pro women's tin now 17 inches.

Longest match, 170 minutes, played beteen Leo Au and Shawn DeLierre.

2016

Nour El Sherbini wins the 1st of 7 women's World titles.

InteractiveSQUASH front walls launched.

WSF changes name of Racketball to Squash57.

2017

Equal prize money for men and women for almost all of the World Series events.

2018

Squash is a showcase sport at the Youth Olympic Games.

2019

1st $1m prize event is M/W World championship in Chicago, USA.

World Squash Library starts.

2021

USA national centre opens in Philadelphia.

2022

PSA rankings move from monthly to weekly.

2023

IOC include squash in the 2028 Olympic Games in Los Angeles.

2024

1st time M/W World Team championships staged together.

IMAGE NOTES

Source:

BVH = collection Bas van Hoorn

SL = taken/supplied by photographer Steve Line

WSL = World Squash Library

Many WSL images were provided by courtesy of individuals and organisations. Every effort has been made to ensure the accuracy of attribution of all images, but if errors have been made, please contact the WSL.

Numbering:

Number = page number

t/m/b = place on page (top/middle/bottom)

1/2/3/4etc = place within t/m/b, from left to right

For example:

49b3 means the third illustration from the left, in the bottom part, of page 49.

CHAPTER 1 (BEFORE SQUASH)

Books: BVH 9t 16m

Equipment: BVH 9b2 13t1 15b1 23m

Original artwork: BVH 12t 23b1

Original engravings/woodcuts: BVH 8t/b 9m/b1 10m1(there were several tennis courts in this area, so its exact location is uncertain)10b 11t/b 12m/b 13t2/b 14t/b2 15t 16b1/b2 17 18m 19t 20m/b1 21b 22b1/b2

Original photographs: BVH 15b2 19b1/b2(glass plate negative) 21t/m2 22m

Trophies/tokens: BVH 10m2 14b1 16t 17b1/b2 20b2(provenance: Weldon family estate; Napoleon Wellington exhibition 1969, Castletown House Kildare, cat.no.142)

Various: BVH 21m1(printed postcard; strangely the Calcutta Racket Club possibly owns its name to a bird, the racket tail) 23b2(cap)

CHAPTER 2 (pre1920)

Books/programmes: BVH 29b 35t1/t2/m2/m3 42t/m 43b1 44t **WSL** 29b 35m3

Equipment: **BVH** 32b1/b2 38t/b(originally contained five dividers) 39t1/t2/t3(found together)

Original engravings/woodcuts: BVH 26m/b(there is some debate if Hart Dyke built three or four squash courts at Harrow) 27t2 34b 37t1/t2 39b 45m(the depicted Olympic was almost identical)

Original photographs: **BVH** 27t1(glass plate negative of G.E. Brown Morisson, Harrow c1882) 29t 30b 36b 40 41b2 44m/b

Printed photos: **BVH** 27b(the courts from 1865 were apparently built in two rows, parallel to the side wall of the rackets court, one row of fives courts, one row of squash courts, with an alley in between). 28m/b2(Cherwell Hall) 33 34m1/m2 35m1/b1 37m/b 42b 43t1/t2/t3/m1/m2/m3/b2 45t(modern postcard) 45b1 **WSL** 28t(some have even suggested that squash was invented at Elstree, before finding its way to Harrow, but no proof was ever found) 30t 31m/b1/b2 36m 41b1 45b2

Trophies/medals: BVH 28b1 31t 35b2 38m 41t/m

CHAPTER 3 (1920s)

Books/programmes: **BVH** 48t/b 50b1 **WSL** 50b1 62b

Equipment: **BVH** 49b1(ball name digitally edited) 49b2 50b2 54b1(originally racket head more rounded; donated by Bert Armstrong whose squash collection is on permanent display at the Kooyong Lawn Tennis Club, Australia) 60t1 61t2/b1/b2

Original photographs: **BVH** 50b3 51 55t 56(signature digitally removed) 60t2/m/b 62t/m 63b1

Printed photos: **BVH** 49t1/t2/m 52t/m/b 53t/m/b1/b2 54b2 55b1 57b1/b2 58t/m 59t1/t2/b **WSL** 54m1/b2 63m1/m2/b2

Trophies/medals: **BVH** 48m(medal awarded to K Gandar-Dower in 1930) 55b2 57m 58b 59m 61t1/m

CHAPTER 4 (1930s)

Books/programmes: BVH 68m 69t1 73b1/b2 77t1/t2/m/b1/b2 82b2 **WSL** 68m 73b1 77m/b1

Equipment: BVH 76b1/b2 78m1/m2 81m 82t/m/b1(grip not original)

Original photographs: BVH 66(signature digitally removed) 67t(signature digitally removed) 68t 70m2 72 74t/m/b 76t 80b 83t1/m

Printed photos: BVH 67m2 69t2/m 70m1/b1/b2 73t 76m 77t3 78t/b 79b 80t 81t/b1/b3 83t2 **WSL** 67m1 71 75 83b

Trophies/medals: BVH 68b 73m 79t (info supplied by Richard Gray)

Various: BVH 69b(telegram) 73b2(cartoon) 81b2(card)

CHAPTER 5 (1940s/50s)

Books/programmes: BVH 89b1 92m2 95b2 96m 101m2/b2/b3 **WSL** 88b1 96m 100m2

Equipment: BVH 95b1 96t 98b 101b1(donated by Bert Armstrong)

Original artwork: BVH 97b

Original photographs: BVH 86t/m 87m 88t/b2 89b2 90 91b2 93 94m 95m 97m 101m1 **WSL** 91b1 94b 96b 97t

Printed photos: BVH 86b 89m 98m 100b 101t1 **WSL** 87b 92b 95t 99 100t/m1 101t2

Trophies/medals: BVH 89t

Various: BVH: 92m1(advertisement board)

CHAPTER 6 (1960s)

Books/programmes: BVH 116m **WSL** 112b1 116t/m 121b2

Equipment: BVH 105t 106t1/t2/t3/b1/b2 109b1 116b

Original artwork: BVH 108m 118b

Original photographs: BVH 105b 108b 110t 111t 112m 114 115m 119 121m/b1 **WSL** 104t/b 105m 109b2 110b 111m 113t/b 118t

Printed photos: BVH 106m/b3/b4 109t 111b1/b2/b3/b4 **WSL** 107 109m 113m 115b 117 118m1/m2 120b1/b2

Various: BVH 112b2(badge) 120m(advertisement board)

CHAPTER 7 (1970s)

Books/programmes: BVH 127b1 128t 131b2 **WSL** 127b1 128t 131b2 134m 135t 141t

Equipment: BVH 127m 131m 133b2 141b

Original artwork: BVH 141m

Original photographs: BVH 127b2 131t 132 133b1 134t 136b 137t/m 138b1 139t1 **SL** 124m 126 127t 130t 133t 134b2 137b2 138t **WSL** 124b 128m/b 130m/b1 134b1 135b1/b2 136t1 137m/b1 139b2 140t/m

Printed photos: BVH 131b1 **WSL** 125 129 130b2 136t2 138b2 139t2/b1 140b

CHAPTER 8 (1980s)

Books/programmes: BVH 149b **WSL** 149b 152b 154m/b

Equipment: BVH 146b2 155 158t1/t2/m1/m2/b 159t1/t2/t3/m1/m2/b

Original photographs: SL 144 145t/b1/b2 146t/m2/b1 147t/m1/b1 148t/m/b1/b2/b3 149t/m1/m2 150t 151 152t/m 153t/m/b 155t/m 156t/b1 157t/m/b 160t1 161m **WSL** 156b1 161b2

Printed photos: WSL 146m1 150b 154t 156b2 160t2/b1/b2 161t/b1

Various: WSL 147m2(stamp) 147b2(scoresheet) 160t3(letter)

CHAPTER 9 (1990s)

Books/programmes: WSL 165b2 171b2 173t/m3 179b1/b2

Equipment: BVH 167t1/t2/m1/m2/m3 169t/b1 172t

Original photographs: SL 164m/b 165m/b1 166t/m/b 168t/m 169m2 170 171m/b1 174 175t/m/b 176t/m1/m/b1/b2 178t1/m1/m2/m3/m4/b1/b2 179t 180 181t1/t3/m1/m2/b1 **WSL** 165t 168b 169m1 173m1/m2 179b3 180b1 181t2/b2

Printed photos: WSL 169b2 177 178t2 180b2

CHAPTER 10 (2000s)

Books/programmes: WSL 191m 194t1/t2 199t1

Equipment: BVH 186t 191b 194m/b

Original photographs: SL 184 185t/m/b 186m/b1 187b 188m/b 189t1/t2/b1/b2 190 191t 192t/m/b 193t1/t2/m/b1/b2 196t/m/b 197t/m/b 198t/m/b1/b2 199t2/m1 **WSL** 187t1/t2/m1/m2

Printed photos: WSL 186b2 189b3 195t/m1/m2 199m2/b

CHAPTER 11 (2010s/20s)

Books/programmes: WSL 210m/b 212t/m/b1 214m 221b

Equipment: BVH 209m1 223b2

Original photographs: SL 202 203t/m/b 204t/m/b 205t/m/b 206t1/t2/m/b 207t/m1/m2/b 208t/b 209m2/b 210t 214t/b 215t/m/b 216m 217t/m 219t1/t2/m/b 220 221t/m 222t/b 223t/b1 224 225t/m/b 226t/m/b 227t/m

Printed photos: WSL 211 212b2 213t/m/b 216b(cartoon by David Banks) 217b 218t/m1/m2/b 223m1/m2 227b

INDEX

Note: Events are not indexed in terms of results, and organisations when mentioned in general terms.